# Isak Dinesen / Karen Blixen

# ISAK DINESEN/ KAREN BLIXEN

## The Work and The Life

### by

# Aage Henriksen

**Translated by William Mishler**
**Introduction by Poul Houe**

ST. MARTIN'S PRESS
NEW YORK

The essays "Karen Blixen and Marionettes" and "The Messenger" appeared in *Det guddomelige barn og andre essays om Karen Blixen*. Copenhagen, Gyldendal, 1965.

"Karen Blixen's Place in Modern European Literature" appeared in *Blixeniana*. Copenhagen, Karen Blixen Selskapet, 1978.

"The Empty Space Between Art and Church" appeared in *Karen Blixen / Isak Dinesen, Tradition, Modernity and Other Ambiguities*, Conference Proceedings, University of Minnesota, 1985.

"The Guardian of the Threshold" and "At Rungstedlund" appeared in *De ubaendige*. Copenhagen, Gyldendal, 1984.

ISAK DINESEN/KAREN BLIXEN. Copyright © 1988 by Gyldendalske Boghandel. Translation copyright © 1988 by St. Martin's Press. Introduction copyright © 1988 by Poul Houe. All rights reserved. Printed in the United States of America. No part of this book may be used or reproduced in any manner whatsoever without written permission except in the case of brief quotations embodied in critical articles or reviews. For information, address St. Martin's Press, 175 Fifth Avenue, New York, N.Y. 10010.

*Design by H. Roberts*

Library of Congress Cataloging-in-Publication Data

Henriksen, Aage.
    Isak Dinesen/Karen Blixen / by Aage Henriksen.
        p. cm.
    ISBN 0-312-01777-4
    1. Dinesen, Isak, 1885–1962.  2. Authors, Danish—20th century—
Biography.  I. Title.
PT8175.B545Z699 1988
839.8′1372—dc19
[B]                                                          87-36715

First Edition
10 9 8 7 6 5 4 3 2 1

# Contents

# Isak Dinesen / Karen Blixen

# Aage Henriksen—
## A Humanistic Critic
### Poul Houe

The fact that Karen Blixen/Isak Dinesen (1885–1962) has exerted considerable influence on English-speaking audiences seems well evidenced; and yet, it appears to be a matter of controversy. Her reputation, for example in the United States, is of long standing and has been certified by remarkable numbers of scholarly publications over the last decades. Similarly, the quantity of Dinesen's books sold or checked out of libraries, in particular since the 1985 premiere of Sydney Pollack's movie *Out of Africa*, seems to indicate great interest in this author and her works among the general public. Nevertheless, there are prominent critics, including Danish professor Aage Henriksen (b. 1921), who point to a different scenario: Isak Dinesen's writings being poetry for poets and a few selected critics, not for every Tom, Dick, and Harry. Moreover, as regards the academic experts of this establishment, their scholarly credentials most likely have as little impact on the cultural scene at large as they allegedly had upon Isak Dinesen herself.

From the standpoint of sociology of literature, the latter scenario is interesting because, above and beyond statistics, it sets a standard of deep personal experience and intellectual commitment, so characteristic of Aage Henriksen's essays on Dinesen, as the foremost prerequisite for approaching her famous tales. "Not reading but experience is what makes the difference," says Henriksen about how to read Isak Dinesen at the end of an article in this volume. Like his other pronouncements it sounds simple, but it has proven a more demanding and challenging guideline than most 'procedures' for coping with the author and her works. To make the inspiration stemming from this notion of literature available to the greatest possible number of non-Danish students of Dinesen has been the prime intention behind the present selection of Henriksen's articles on Isak Dinesen. At the same time, the volume at hand constitutes the only comprehensive book-length study written by Aage Henriksen exclusively on Isak Dinesen.

There is yet another reason for presenting this critic in English translation and for having the presentation center on Isak Dinesen. In the works of his American colleagues—from Eric Johannesson and Robert Langbaum to Thomas Whissen and Judith Thurman—Aage Henriksen stands out as the respected friend of Isak Dinesen as well as the pioneering Dinesen scholar. However, in reciprocating these gestures of scholarly acknowledgment, Henriksen, for the most part, has been unobtrusive, to say the least (see, for instance, his guarded praise in a lengthy review of the Danish edition Langbaum's book, *The Gayety of Vision*, in the daily *"Information"* Nov. 17, 1964). Unlike some of his existentialist followers in Denmark, Henriksen readily joined in the Anglo-American advocacy and deployment of New Criticism—at least to the extent this critical school of thought enabled him to separate the literary work from its author's personality. But as opposed to most English and American critics, *his* interest in the separation lay not so much in the text as in the personality, the latter following the former as a shadow.

Dinesen's personality encompassed tremendous human experience, and elicited her friend's preoccupation with himself as it called his attention to works in which this experience of human complexity and wholeness was profoundly reflected. Once under the spellbinding influence of Isak Dinesen's world, Henriksen admittedly allowed it to oust the competing genius of Søren Kierkegaard, the subject of his doctoral thesis, from his active sphere of interest. Or, rather, the abstractions and conceptualizations inherent in Kierkegaard inevitably cut a poor figure in Henriksen's mind compared with the sense of personal reality he experienced in meeting Dinesen. Kierkegaard put aside, Isak Dinesen clearly assumed the leading position among Henriksen's elective affinities, and never did he stroke New Criticism against the hair more deeply than in her case. It is fair to say, therefore, that his writings on this international writer represent the ideal gate for, say, American students of literature anxious to explore a familiar framework on new terms. Henriksen's professional subjectivity is a synthesis of literary scholarship and criticism, and offers an intriguing perspective on the American critical canon, not an obscure European addition to its table of contents.

That literary figures other than Dinesen—besides Kierkegaard, Goethe, and Ibsen, Professor Henriksen's scholarly repertoire consists chiefly of Danish lyrical poets of the early and late nineteenth century—are not mentioned in the present volume is warranted insofar as it clears the sight for one of his most captivating but not one of his most transparent compositional layouts. At the same time it is a shortcoming; these absent characters are *conspicuous* by their absence in the simple sense that Henriksen's approach to their life and work came to fruition especially in consequence of Isak Dinesen's influence. People like the transitional and transitory cosmopolitan poet Jens Baggesen became explicable in the wake of his understanding of her, partly because they traveled the same ways she had depicted, and to leave them out afterward is somehow to delete what she indelibly brought to bear. It also truncates the significance of Henriksen's meetings with the poets, his exposition of the interrelationship between the nature of human illusions and human passions. This interrelationship can be described directly in humanistic terms as an alternative to modernistic perceptions and views, and it works in two directions: reaching out for functional connections in the actual society, and extending into moral norms and intentions behind human endeavors in everyday life as well as into notions of historical and literary pursuits.

While the scope of these selected articles has been narrowed down to a monographic treatment of Isak Dinesen so as to secure the sharpness of its focus, this introduction, conversely, is an attempt to contextualize Professor Henriksen's humanistic "project" within its wide range of merits. It is not an attempt to bolster the author's ultimate reconstruction of tradition; but it *is* an attempt to offer tentatively an opportunity to compare favorably with the image of a scarecrow, which has occasionally been allotted by ideology critiques and other antitraditional deconstructions within their contextualizations and frames of interpretation. I believe that in humanistic studies critics with an interest as well as some skepticism at stake are deserving of maximal inspiration and provocation stemming from this body of cultural criticism. Aage Henriksen's essays on Dinesen are central in this respect, and the following sketch of his production and ideas at large is to facilitate especially the unprepared reader's appreciation of this centrality.

Aage Henriksen's academic breakthrough dates back to 1949–55 when he was a visiting professor of Danish language and literature at Lund University in Sweden. *Methods and Results of Kierkegaard Studies in Scandinavia: A Historical and Critical Survey* (1951) was written in preparation for his doctoral thesis on Kierkegaard's novels, *Kierkegaards romaner* (1954), in which he unassumingly contributes original solutions to a variety of problems posed by Kierkegaard's pseudonymous works, not by entertaining a discussion of the problems of pseudonymity in general but by interpreting three specific texts as aesthetic totalities—or novels. With reference to rather informal notions of aesthetic "holism" (based on vaguely defined appropriations of New Criticism), Henriksen sets out conceptual analyses of Kierkegaardian catchwords (e.g., "gentagelse" and "angst") leading up, eventually, to the fundamental formula for Kierkegaard's philosophy of epoch. In doing so, Henriksen succeeds in describing the principal characters and their existential positions between spontaneity and infinite reflection as slightly individualized "masks of character" conceived in the light of contemporary "problematics of liberty." Without being a conspicuously traditional academic treatise, Henriksen's dissertation is by far the most conventional monograph on its author's list of publications. By its definition of topic, its orderly composition, and its analytical procedures, his book was in tune with the novel trends of New Criticism as they applied to the study of literary genres in Nordic philology around 1950. Notwithstanding its fine expositions of Kierkegaard's dialectical aesthetics, this book was not to remain its author's guide for very long.

The reason for this was Isak Dinesen, whom Henriksen met after he had lectured on her first two collections of tales and later published his papers in a small book entitled *Karen Blixen og marionetterne* (*Karen Blixen and Marionettes*) in 1952. In his correspondence with Dinesen, underlying his chapter "At Rungstedlund" in the present volume and published in its entirety in *Blixeniana* (1985), some of the first exchanges between the two are concerned, precisely, with Kierkegaard as he compared to Dinesen. The difference between these two personalities, in Henriksen's view, are obvious; yet they do converge in an intimate and primitive conception of everydayness. Isak Dinesen even attempts to declare a special feeling of personal connection with Kierkegaard, although she has to admit that while she could "fall on Shakespeare's neck," she could, at the most, "fall on Kierkegaard's breast," meaning "resent his opinions"! She concludes by saying that what Kierkegaard and Henriksen know in theory—about the paradox of the demonic, about the individual and the universal, and so on—she knows from personal experience. From that time onward, Henriksen in his letters and interviews, and in his general orientation as a critic, follows suit and becomes detached, as was Dinesen, from Kierkegaard's sphere of influence and Hegelian discourse. As a matter of fact, one of his many objections to Robert Langbaum's cavalier book on Dinesen's art is aimed at its false contention that the modern writer of fiction was directly influenced by the nineteenth-century philosopher.

The extent to which Henriksen henceforth became dependent on (what developed into a friendship with) Isak Dinesen is convincingly documented in this book. The expressions that this intellectual relationship assumed in some of his letters verge on the pathetic and have, indeed, proven vulnerable to ridicule; more important, however, is to notice how they testify to Henriksen's self-comprehension and future orientation in life and work. Not only does Isak Dinesen perform as his guardian angel; he even tends to see the cultural crisis of Denmark in the 1950s in the mirror of his country's inability to wholeheartedly accept her in its midst. What "modern" and "modernity" mean to him becomes a typical matter of ongoing discussions between the two, and in the same manner the haunting question of everyday reality and what it signifies finds its most thought-provoking solutions in her presence. The latter in a striking contrast to modern science with its efforts systematically to dissociate humaneness from everyday situations and language, from totality and *anschauung* (a typical word with no equivalent term in English), and from the individual and its individuality.

In the opening chapter of his doctoral thesis, Henriksen explained to his reader how careful attention to (characteristic) details prevented him from pursuing the higher purpose of literary study as it reveals itself only when the very tension and contrast between the narrative voices of interrelated works gets put under scrutiny. What had to be excluded from consideration for purely academic reasons in this early book is precisely what constitutes the rest of his production. For example, both *Den rejsende: Otte kapitler om Jens Baggesen og hans tid* (*The Traveller: Eight Chapters* on *Jens Baggesen and His Time*, 1961) and *Det guddom-melige barn og andre essays om Karen Blixen* (*The Divine Child and Other Essays on Karen Blixen*, 1965) are wide-ranging and intertwined compositions, each in its own right, as suggested in their respective subtitles. The former about the volatile Danish-German eighteenth–nineteenth-century poet is indirectly but basically composed on Henriksen's idea of a tension between Goethe and Dinesen; and the latter, on Dinesen herself, is in part about Thomas Mann and in part about Danish symbolist lyric poet Sophus Claussen. In his essay on Claussen, the last and largest contribution to this book-length study of Dinesen, she herself enters the stage only a few pages from the last period. And Henriksen's most recent essay on Claussen (1986)[1] is conceived in a similar manner as the third chapter out of four inserts in a discussion of Dinesen (with an implicit view to the others on Claussen).

To do justice, within a short preface, to Henriksen's writings by applying oneself to their serpentine compositions is not an easy task. Fortunately, his collection of essays from 1964 to 1974, *Den intellektuelle* (*The Intellectual*, 1974), is easier to handle and outline. No less subtly put together, these pieces are both shorter and more autonomously struc-tured; furthermore, both incorporate the bulk of his artistic and intellectual favorites and display his increasing absorp-tion in extrapersonal matters. Altogether, these essays on Ibsen, Freud, and everyday reality can be looked on as har-bingers of the contents of Henriksen's latest book *De ubaen-dige* (*The Indomitable*, 1984), from which the remaining two essays on Isak Dinesen have been included in the present translation.

Obviously, it is totality and the search for a frame of interpretation encompassing artistic expressions of such to-tality (be they normative or norm-breaking expressions) that trigger Aage Henriksen's essayistic strategies. Only seem-ingly is this a paradox. Consider, for example, the potential interplay between the two short essays "Love and Seman-tics" and "Baggesen, the European." In the former, Hen-riksen says of Goethe that if used correctly he renders the opposition between monism and dualism superfluous inasmuch as he contrived to "take into personal possession the inner world which restraints or inhibitions had evoked in him, and the outer world which remained accessible to his senses and desires." Spirituality—or love, as it were—occurs when and where sensuality is being thwarted; and yet, spirituality and sensuality are not without affinity.

For Jens Baggesen, who was destined, owing to his geographical and mental rootlessness, to examine European Man from bottom to top, a compatible attitude to spiritual and sensual experiences was out of the question. Says Henriksen, "His passport gave him access to all of the world, but his own heart." Baggesen went many places to learn about himself and the world, but he fell short of finding a single place where he would like to stay and where his learning experiences could combine into knowledge. Hence European Man in embryo gets divided into two halves, the poet and the politician, before he is even born. The obstacles overcome by Goethe's harmonious concord are seen to overcome Jens Baggesen in satirical discord. Their two lives are mutually related as fulfillment to potential, or as one "essay" accomplishing another.

The psychology behind this moral complexity is unveiled in Henriksen's studies of the old Henrik Ibsen's symbolic dramas. Here a basic human selfishness appears in the perfect disguise of reliable ideals; in reality the individual's unruly nature behaves even more shatteringly when subdued in this sanctimonious manner. In this situation Ibsen's language takes the visible plot of his drama back to its original state of human conditions, leaving the reader and spectator with an impression of inveterate ambiguousness, which was only inadvertently part and parcel of the author's moral(istic) layout. Once a fact, it evokes, nonetheless, a subtle and dubious delight on Ibsen's part. When human beings position their desires in the world around them, their dreams come true as a result of others' will, not of their own. Taking into account, intuitively if not deliberately, the elements of risk involved in such dependence, most people (ad)dress their intentions in whatever fashion they find agreeable to the others. An outgoing manipulation with the innermost consequences has been initiated! Or public discourse sequestered for reckless private motives. The old Henrik Ibsen pays heed to what Man says and does only to disclose what passions his words and actions are serving.

Unlike the individual depicted in his work, the author does not find fulfillment for passions and desires of his own in the surrounding world. His immediate needs remain undercover while a stronger, artistic desire, in return for his physical want, endows his passion with endurance within the literary context. The illusion that came to the fore as a brutal necessity on the level of plot and human drama appears an elevated virtue on the level of artistic execution. This, according to Henriksen, is a shared experience in Goethe, Kierkegaard, and Blixen, among others.

Insofar as the illusion is a matter of artistic talent and aesthetic totality, this poetics is not in disagreement with the tenets of New Criticism. But insofar as a human drama and a sequence of human experiences are invested and articulated within the same aesthetics, its pronouncements go well beyond what New Criticism has proven capable of accounting for. To Henriksen the role of the literary critic is not simply to share in an author's dismantling of artistic illusions; it is also to restore the connection between these signs of ostensible falsehood and their underlying human passions. This is what makes him a humanistic critic—of high standing and some obsoleteness.

For the literary scholar this means a break with modern science, its disregard for experiences of totality, and its overconcern with special knowledge and terminology. Being the correspondent between the inner passions he serves and the outer topics of which he knows from his senses, the modern scientist is a divided character: his passions are disorderly acting on their own, while his sense of subject matter is under the utmost control. In contradistinction to this model of scholarly cognition, Henriksen proposes an admission of passion, intellect, and subject matter to a sphere of mutual influences. The subject of cognition is invited to enter its private world of desires, not by way of introspection but by way of interlocking human thought and action. Thus the subject of cognition here at hand is one's own individuality in a situation where it can be prompted by inner forces responding to outer circumstances.

As regards literature, this means that the canon must once again be read with a view to values to which any work of literature can properly relate in a servant capacity. And that primarily occurs when its reader engrosses herself in such everyday habits, meanings, and thoughts of which people are not in full control. This is where the literary work proves capable of increasing its reader's awareness of the ends of her desires, and where, accordingly, the continuity of tradition may find its future repository. Literature, then, is the one subject matter that essentially includes Man in its definition: Man as the subject *and* object of motivated action. But it must be emphasized how high literature in particular utilizes its respect for everyday reality as a platform for liberation: liberation from external circumstances, and freedom to subject itself to spirituality and its laws; to the lawfulness of imagination.

In Goethe the way in which the world of the senses is both a hindrance and a pathway for the poet and his insights is typified by the way his "proto-plant" shines from behind all individual plants. The poet, in his work, can refer to anything "real," but he only perpetuates "reality" in its relation to human passions (thereby rendering possible the secretion from the total mass of sensations of pure structures of consciousness). The historical dimension of this poetical strategy becomes apparent in Henriksen's principal work *Gotisk tid: Fire litteraere essays* (*Gothic Time: Four Literary Essays*, 1971). The last of these essays deals with the language of composition—types and problems of novels—and it labors to demonstrate how the forms of cognitive transformation, not the forms of exterior reality, are the objectives of artistic configuration. In fact, the exterior reality itself is in a trans-form-ing position or, in the form of a mirror, reflecting the inner forms of consciousness (at least so long as modern scientific imperialism has not seized every piece of real matter and deprived the psyche of its correlate in the outside world; at that point a new kind of novel enters the stage lest the abolished effect of the traditional mirror fall into absolute oblivion).

Since the Middle Ages human passions have not been granted indefinite redemption in this world. The individual has been isolated in his transcendental destiny. With the introduction of humanistic education, so-called *bildung*, it became possible, however, to discern a finite solution to the inherited problem of Christian indefiniteness. An incipient merger of faith and knowledge forms the backbone of a ubiquitous harmony resting essentially, throughout the early nineteenth century, on Goethe's trans-gressing faculties. This point of time, in turn, becomes the point of departure for Henriksen's indefatigable efforts to put the quest for human liberation into a contemporary frame of mind. His rewriting of tradition into a humanistic model of communication reasserts the poetic codes for liberation from human passions in a way that does not comply with today's criteria of scientific verification. Instead of being loyal to modernism, his practice reminds of the *bildungstradition* itself as it transferred transcendental capacity from the realm of God to the responsibility of Man. Even then the concomitant emergence of confidence and fidelity were aberrant by novel scientific norms and standards.

With secularization progressing into the Modern Breakthrough in Nordic literature, the predominant Christian view of history was replaced by a philosophical view of human freedom. Yet the individual personality and its everydayness somehow were left in limbo. While more traditional humanists proposed a revival of unified cultural norms with the individual at its center, more critical humanists readily laid the blame for current decays on the very same traditional culture (so saturated with invisible images and refined personalities, and yet so oppressive of reality and tangible facts). A shared awareness of human fragmentation, and a shared emergency appeal to cooperative democracies, interest groups, and other forms of objective reality (representing various clusters of living fragments), nonetheless contributed a concordance of humanistic pledges to solve the crisis in question.

Meanwhile, the whole gamut of *modernists* revolted against the same fragmentation by claiming that their experiences of artistic production be granted absolute authority. To sacrifice one's empirical and social ego for the benefit of artistic integrity became the desired stigma of these modernists. Only artistic subjects in charge of endless transgression into form-demanding nothingness would be granted homestead in these projects, notwithstanding the apparent absurdity that their revolts against fragmentation must capitalize on various parts of former Man.

Aage Henriksen's location of Isak Dinesen's position within this dichotomy between tradition and modernity is available for scrutiny in the present volume and requires no further commentary. His review of the full scenario in itself is captivating, while his vested interest in its traditional part might prove to be merely thought-provoking. It is fortunate, therefore, that his critical theory of humanistic holism (extending beyond the confines of science versus art and socialism versus humanism) has produced and provoked its own critical response.

Aage Henriksen was named professor of Nordic literature at Copenhagen University in 1969. That was the heyday of the Danish student revolt that went on to leave deep impressions upon the humanities in that country. Professor Henriksen was known as an inspiring lecturer and was heralded, initially, as "a scholar who has taken the consequences of understanding how difficult it is to really know anything," to cite only one of his outspoken students and apologists.[2] If people expected a viable alternative to the old professorial authority, and someone alien to the ideological confusion of academic freedom with humanistic scholarship "free" of values, their new professor undoubtedly came up to their expectations. He openly announced his readiness to take responsibility for such future developments and improvements of his field. But left-wing university and general politics among student and junior faculty were soon to raise more radical expectations of which Henriksen was considered to fall short.

Shortly before his appointment to the chair in Copenhagen, Henriksen together with Johan Fjord Jensen, his equally prominent colleague and philosophical adversary at Aarhus University, founded Denmark's most influential literary journal in recent times, *Kritik* (*Critique*, 1967 ff.). It soon became an enlivening meeting ground for talented representatives of scholarly, pedagogical, artistic, and critical milieus, and it served as a midwife for a variety of upcoming trends and controversies along with new interpretational propositions and strategies typical of these years' productive and animated intellectual upheavals. After three years of fruitful coeditorship and polemic dialogues between Fjord Jensen and Henriksen, and with increasing politization and polarization between their respective "constituencies," *Kritik* was facing rather intractable editorial complications. Eventually they turned it away from the positions at Aarhus to become, instead, a more permanent and exclusive forum for the Henriksen "estate" at Copenhagen.

Johan Fjord Jensen, the foremost Danish historian of New Criticism in the 1960s, in the 1970s devoted his intellectual energies to launch, in typical collaboration with his students, some major research projects on mass culture in comic strips and magazines, more and more firmly rooted in Marxist ideology critique. Later he was to become the prime mover of Denmark's largest literary history project, that too on Marxist grounds, published in nine volumes in the early 1980s. Aage Henriksen, by comparison, no less typically gathered his followers in Copenhagen around projects with partly comparable breadth and scope, and yet with entirely different priorities, different methods, and a different degree of individualized collaboration. *Den erindrende Faun* (*The Reminiscent Faun*, 1968) is edited by Henriksen et al., and it consists of articles mainly on nineteenth-century Danish poets demonstrating, altogether, the gradual breakdown of Romantic idealism and the consequences thereof in Ibsen and others. The mechanics of this collision between imagination and reality conforms with Henriksen's theory of human passions and desires being deprived of natural outlets. Thanks to various impediments, sublimation takes over and deposits the original sensations in the form of erotic patterns of destiny, spiritual complications or composition accessible to interpretation. In *Ideologihistorie* (*History of Ideology*), also masterminded by Henriksen and published in four volumes in the late 1970s, the basic principles are in line with the same program; yet on the one hand its focus is manifestly on "ideology," on the other its material includes a much broader spectrum of texts, and its span of time has been expanded from the nineteenth century to cover even neighboring centuries (1770–1970) and in principle all centuries since the dawn of Danish literature.

To give an impression of the aforementioned gap between Aage Henriksen's projects and the interests associated with ideological matters in the projects shepherded by Fjord Jensen, suffice it to point out now how "ideology" is being used in Henriksen's context. To him the necessities and the everyday reality of people define the conditions under which they receive "ideology" in the form of superior structures and value systems imperative to their lives (and transmitted from outside or above the places where they live). Over the centuries, and in high literature, the focal point of this imposition on human life has shifted from ideals of family (before 1300) to ideals of King and Christianity (1100–1870) and on to ideals of science and society (since 1870); in low literature, referred to as ideology critique, and at any time, the changing positions of these official norms have been subjected to criticism, skepticism, satire, and so on. Obviously this classification of ideological positions and ideology critique is at odds with the Marxist philosophy of class and class struggle. To specify its compatibilities is somewhat easier since Henriksen's characterization of the nineteenth century elaborates on his words about Goethe's proto-plant:

> With the idea of organicism a new world separated itself from the old world. . . . Key words such as *nature, development, organism, personality, people, history, subconsciousness, inspiration, genius,* were coined and given the worth of which they are still worthy today . . . Scholarly trends like evolution and psychoanalysis, and political philosophies like nazism and marxism have all emerged as the result of changing structures within the Romantic ideas of organicism.

Henriksen has been harshly criticized for vaguely speculating in *analogical* argumentation allowing for reactionary, manipulative, and repressive maintenance of social peace. "As long as this technique is efficient, no gas chambers are needed," concludes one of his critics.[3] Henriksen's acceptance of tradition and wholeness—if only as a challenge—has been construed as subversive self-indulgence or, at best, as an acceptance of the world as good enough as is. A poetics of passions in lieu of a politics of passions, to remember another critique.[4]

The intellectual climate today has effaced some of these polemics, and it ought to be possible for the reader of this book to review dispassionately the most fundamental problems embedded in Henriksen's discourse—all the more so because its basic understanding of how passions change originated in Isak Dinesen and her influence upon him. Irrespective of the reader's conclusion in this matter, he or she is likely to agree that Professor Henriksen has accomplished a demanding challenge to followers and opponents alike. In this sense he has definitely removed the wrinkles of literary study. In yet another sense, in his style, he has successfully preserved them. His writing is spiritual in its simplicity and subtle in its humor; or, in the sense of his own words about his former teacher, the late Ejnar Thomsen, whose posthumous articles he coedited and prefaced in 1956, "his style is incredibly alive . . . honest, intimate, and odd."[5]

To further relate Henriksen to mental and "mentorial" forerunners makes little sense in a brief introduction largely to a new readership. One whose originality, intellectual format, and subject-oriented thinking does come to mind is Danish theologian K. E. Løgstrup and his monumental work on *Metaphysics* (I–IV; 1976–78). However, Løgstrup's study of language, culture, and art is indebted to a notion of Creation and Nature that is not shared by Henriksen, and that might also give an American reader some false associations to humanism as a special branch of modern agnosticism. So, let me instead refer to the statement that concludes the above-mentioned portrayal of Ejnar Thomsen. Unlike the previous reference to Henriksen's stylistic oddity, with its touch of dubious compliment, the following pronouncement is unambiguously pertinent to his own character as a scholar and writer: "He was a man of great dispositions, a sincere and serious human being troubled by thoughts, for whom depth was deep. It is the man which the books are meant to keep in mind and preserve."[6] I believe that Aage Henriksen, this humanistic critic, is particularly well served in this collection of his essays on Isak Dinesen.

—Poul Houe

# Notes

1. Aage Henricksen, "Svaueteden. Et essay om Sophus Claussen," in *Fra Nexø til Saxo* (Copenhagen, C. A. Reitzels Forlay, 1986).
2. Erik A. Nielsen, "Videnskab og videnskab: Portrøt," *Information*, March 18, 1968.
3. Carl Erik Bay, "Om organisme-analogien," *Information*, October 26, 1973.
4. Jette Lundbo Levy, "Traditionens guru eller drifternes politik," *Vindrosen* 6 (1970): 59–66.
5. Aage Henriksen, "Ejnar Thomsen," in Ejnar Thomsen, *Digteren og Kaldet: Efterladte Skrifter* (Copenhagen, Gyldendal, 1957), p. 11.
6. Ibid., p. 14.

# CHAPTER 1

# Karen Blixen and Marionettes

## 1. *Seven Gothic Tales*

The qualities that have led to Karen Blixen's literary fame are the first ones to strike the readers of her stories. The exquisite and refined narrative manner and the mysterious and fantastic elements of their plots have given her readers a somewhat intimidating impression of her: Karen Blixen as the aristocrat and sybil in Danish literature, the great anachronism who manages to combine old culture with archaic unculture. But this portrait reveals only half the truth, and it suffers a bit from banality. There is much spirit in Karen Blixen's writings, but not so much witchcraft as people have tended to impute to them; she enchants without bewitching. And her aristocratic manner never outweighs her piety.

One of the chief reasons why Karen Blixen has a dazzling and disorienting effect on her readers is because they take for literary sophistication what is basically her personal viewpoint. In her tales, stories and anecdotes are arranged in layers, one on top of the other, and the innermost kernel

of any of her tales is never a moral principle but rather
another smaller story or an image. Compositional lines never
meet in a point but come together to form a figure. This is
a consistent characteristic in everything she has written—
including her book of memoirs, *Out of Africa*. It was in the
light of an image or through a symbol that she attempted to
understand her situation in Africa when she encountered
adversity. This means that for her it is not the concept but
rather myth and portent that are the primary spiritual en-
tities capable of revealing humanity's basic conditions.

In her writing Blixen gives most weight to the symbol
of the marionette and the biblical myth of the Fall. Historically speaking, it seems that it was the discovery of the
marionette play's perspective that provided the impulse for
her mature work. In 1926, almost ten years prior to any of
the works for which she was to become known, she published
a little play, *The Revenge of Truth*. It is a short marionette
comedy that contains in essence the thoughts which later
will receive much larger orchestration in her famous tales.
This is not to say that the works *The Revenge of Truth* and
*Seven Gothic Tales* or her second collection, *Winter's Tales*,
are merely variations of the same theme. We might try to
give a picture of how these three works are related to the
symbol of the marionette by recalling a well-known advertisement: a picture of a little girl carrying a package of oat-
meal under her arm; on her package, a picture of the same
little girl; and on that package, the hint of another picture
of the same little girl. Just as the smallest little girl provides
the seed of the picture, so to speak, and the largest little
girl the outline of the whole, so is the marionette the seed
from which sprang *The Revenge of Truth*. It also forms the
delimiting line for the fates depicted in *Winter's Tales*.

The marionette had been used as a symbol in literature
before Karen Blixen. Heinrich von Kleist's small, marvel-
ously witty dialog in *On the Marionette Comedy*, for example, provides good background material for reading Blixen.
The narrator of this dialog relates that one day he saw a
famous ballet master in the audience at a marionette theater,

and he wondered how a man used to human dancers could find enjoyment in watching lifeless dolls. When he later poses this question to the ballet master, the latter answers that it is precisely the absence of soul in the marionette that constitutes its great superiority. That the puppet has no soul means that it is impossible for it to pretend to be something that it is not. Because it is purely physical it is entirely subject to mechanical laws. A simple tug on its thread makes it perform rhythmical, dancelike motions—a dance of such indescribable grace and lightness that no human dancer can compete with it. But this is possible on the sole condition that the thread be attached at the requisite point of gravity, something one can do with marionettes but not with a human being, for the point of gravity in the human dancer is the soul, and the ability to coordinate one's soul with the corresponding gravitational point in the motion was lost at the Fall. Now it is only the marionette, pure matter, and God, pure spirit, that possess absolute gracefulness.

Implicit in this profound philosophical joke is the notion that in each human being has been implanted a definition, which it is his questionable privilege to be able actively to reject. Of all beings, only the human is capable of creating himself, of remaking himself according to his own ideas. The witch in Blixen's marionette comedy expresses the same idea with the following words:

> Some people do things they don't want to do, and they forget what they themselves really are. They upset the ideas of Nature, and they make her clear springs muddy, beware of them! In the dark, all night long, the trees in the woods are growing. If there is a wind blowing, the tops of the trees sway in it. Such people as I am talking about, wake at night, become anxious, and feel ashamed when they think about it. . . . The truth is that we are all acting in a marionette comedy, and my children, what is more important than anything else in a marionette comedy is to keep the author's idea clear. It is a secret, one which I nevertheless will tell you, that this is the real happiness which people search for

in other places. And so, my fellow players, keep the author's idea clear, aye, drive it to its utmost conclusion.

In *Out of Africa* there is a short essay entitled "Of Pride" that repeats this idea with fewer images:

> Pride is faith in the idea that God had, when he made us. A proud man is conscious of the idea, and aspires to realize it. He does not strive towards a happiness, or comfort, which may be irrelevant to God's idea of him. His success is the idea of God, successfully carried through, and he is in love with his destiny. As the good citizen finds his happiness in the fulfilment of his duty to the community, so does the proud man find his happiness in the fulfilment of his fate.
>
> People who have no pride are not aware of any idea of God in the making of them, and sometimes they make you doubt that there has ever been much of an idea, or else it has been lost, and who shall find it again? They have got to accept as success what others warrant to be so, and to take their happiness, and even their own selves, at the quotation of the day. They tremble, with reason, before their fate. (P. 271)

The marionette comedy is called *The Revenge of Truth* because the witch who states its underlying idea has put a curse on the tavern where the action takes place to the effect that every lie told therein will become truth before the night has passed. Such is the irony with which Nemesis exercises justice upon bad marionettes.

Karen Blixen kept this little comedy in mind when she began writing her mature works. In "The Roads Round Pisa," the first of the *Seven Gothic Tales*, the play is performed in a puppet theater by a troupe of traveling acrobats; this occurs at a point in the story when several of the characters have a respite from their own affairs and can turn their interest elsewhere. The play holds their attention because its double theme—marionettes subject to Nemesis—shows them an image that they themselves, in larger format, are in the process of inscribing on the landscape around Pisa.

The character in the tale who follows the fresh traces of this inscription, covering in two days' time a year's worth of events and in this way making their outline visible, is Augustus von Schimmelman, a Danish count who in the year 1821 is traveling in Italy. He is a man profoundly confused about his life. He has lost or forgotten the idea God had when he made him, and now he is vainly searching for his own image. For a few days, however, in an *osteria* outside of Pisa, Augustus is temporarily relieved of his invisible burden of unsolved problems by being pressed into service as an extra in the last act of a great drama.

The year before Augustus's arrival a great scandal had occurred in Pisa; mighty passions had been stirred up and then had subsided again. But only in appearance. For a number of the implicated persons the story cannot be forgotten; they are bound to its dark core as to a riddle or a fate. And on the day when Augustus stops at the *osteria* near Pisa, the main actors in the drama are restlessly on the move on the roads surrounding the town, all of them in some way moving toward a resolution. Augustus's role begins when an old lady, Countess Carlotta di Gampocorta, is hurt when her carriage accidentally overturns outside the inn where he has just taken up residence. She is carried inside with a broken arm. Alone with Augustus, she asks him to travel to Pisa, find her granddaughter Rosina, and tell her that her grandmother has broken her right arm and is now ready to give her her blessing. To make her message comprehensible to Augustus, she tells him her story, leading him forward into the complications of a situation that can only really be understood in reverse.

Rosina is not her real granddaughter, but her husband's from his first marriage. His first wife died in childbirth. His daughter had the same fate as her mother: at age seventeen, she, too, died giving birth to a daughter. Now it is the old lady's deepest wish that her step-granddaughter may be spared the fate of her mother and grandmother. When the old Prince

Pozentiani proposed to Rosina, Carlotta did everything in her power to bring the marriage about, for she knew that this rich old man and lover of beauty was incapable, through one of nature's quirks, of being a woman's lover. Rosina, for her part, was flattered to have such a powerful suitor and agreed to the engagement. A short time later, however, she fell passionately in love with her cousin Mario and refused to marry the prince.

Carlotta, suspecting that disaster was about to strike Rosina, warned her that to mention this relationship to her fiancé would put Mario's life in danger, because of the prince's skill with a pistol. To the prince she explained Rosina's sudden reluctance as a passing whim, and thus she forced the marriage to take place. But Rosina, having set her mind on her cousin, decided to use her knowledge of the prince's impotence. Shortly after the wedding, she threatened her husband with a public divorce on the grounds that she was still a virgin and their marriage unconsummated. The prince, terrified at the thought that the bitterest secret of his life would become a topic of public gossip, began plotting against her. She on her side plotted against him. He enlisted the help of his friend, Prince Giovanni, a great lover and lady's man, offering to pay his extensive debts if on a given night he would go to Rosina's bedroom and rape her. Meanwhile Rosina, needing to speak to Mario, gave the slip to the spies whom the prince had set to watch over her by arranging that her friend Agnese come secretly to her bedroom one night and lie in her bed while she has her rendezvous with Mario. Both secret plans got carried out on the same night. A short time later Rosina successfully petitioned the pope to annul her marriage, supporting her case with medical proof of her virginity, and soon afterward she wedded Mario.

Carlotta, unaware of either intrigue, is filled with sorrow and bitterness at the news; the old prince falls down in mortal surprise; and Giovanni believes that he has been involved in a miracle. This is the enigmatic or distorted aspect that the past presents to the actors in the drama when they set out the following year to break the magic spell. Carlotta, who had vowed to bless no marriage of Rosina's other than with the prince so long as she can raise her right arm, has heard that Rosina is pregnant, and she is on her way to Pisa to forgive her and give her blessing. On the way she breaks her right arm. The play is almost over. What God had planned as a little idyll nears its intended conclusion in Mario and Rosina's domestic happiness, but at the same time the revenge of truth is being unleashed upon the stubborn marionettes who have not kept their author's idea clear and who have forced him to make a long, complicated comedy out of an idyll.

The next afternoon, when Augustus stops at another inn outside of Pisa, he finds himself under the same roof as the two princes and the girl, Agnese, and the clock begins to chime for all of them. During a heated and cryptic conversation, Pozentiani accuses his former friend of cheating; Giovanni has nothing to reply, since he believes that God has annulled the effect of his crime. In order to conclude this maddening story he insults the mighty marksman Pozentiani and provokes him into a duel. "A conclusion can be a divine thing," says Pozentiani mildly, as this long period of stasis finally takes a turn toward renewed life and action. The following morning his remark becomes the solemn and literal truth. At the moment when the duel is about to begin, Agnese steps forward and states that she, on the night of the rape, had been lying in Rosina's bed. At once the conspirators grasp how Providence, by the secret little maneuver of tying the two intrigues together, has taken people who were criminals in a human tragedy and made them into fools in a divine comedy. The old prince gives a final outburst of protest and falls down dead; the paid rapist turns burning with repentance and love toward Agnese; and she, with a grand gesture, forgives Giovanni and walks away, leaving him standing where his passion and his circumstances have placed him.

In the last of the *Seven Gothic Tales*, "The Poet," the action is simpler; it has less the lofty, classical air of "The

Roads Round Pisa" and more the gloom of psychic twilight. The double erotic triangle of "The Roads Round Pisa" is simplified to its traditional form. The action takes place around 1836 in the region of Hirscholm; Councillor Mathiesen has Pozentiani's role here but resembles him only in his ruthlessness. The old prince was a character of great magnificence and painfully narrow limitations; he took and he gave with terrible innocence until, in desperation, he overstepped his boundaries and was cast down. The councillor does nothing but take; he is a character for whom all paths lead inward. He has put himself in the role of God for the town of Hirscholm, and he has more or less lived up to it as far as the young poet Anders Kube is concerned. Anders, who is a man with a deep, wild soul that no one understands and who therefore is unable to express himself with any degree of concentrated force, allows himself to be dominated by his Maecenas.

The councillor might have had his way, his stature increasing along with Anders's reputation, had it not been for a captivating widow by the name of Fransine who happened to settle in Hirscholm. The instant she sees Anders she understands his potential, and beneath her deep gaze Anders starts to come to life. The councillor understands nothing of this, but he does grasp that dangerous powers are being unleashed in Anders that must be quickly subdued if he is to retain his position as Maecenas. He decides to keep Anders under control by having him marry the sweet and charming widow. He pursues this plan until one day he happens to discover that Fransine too hides great reserves of imagination and passion beneath her quiet, doll-like exterior. At once he changes his plans and proposes to her himself. To Anders he now assigns the role of unhappy lover as an equally good means of control. Fransine complies. She spent her youth in a ghetto and is not used to fighting. She does what people expect of her and lives her real life in dreams. But Anders, who now understands his purpose in life, resolves to drown himself on the day of her wedding. She has called him to life, and now he would rather die than go back to his

former existence. Thus the councillor's second plan is doomed
to failure, since its primary purpose had been to keep Anders
under his control.

Meanwhile, two events occur that are about to transform fiasco into catastrophe. The first is that Fransine falls
as deeply in love with Anders as he has with her; like him,
she feels reborn, as if emerging from the shadows. The second event is that the councillor is composing his third plan:
having played with the young couple like a pair of marionettes, he now intends to wring the utmost from them. He
arranges for them to meet in a final, heartbreaking lovers'
rendezvous on the night before his and Fransine's wedding.
He does not, in so many words, tell them to meet, but he is
so adroit at dropping subtle hints that at last they think they
have come up with the plan themselves. The councillor does
not so much wish to control their thoughts as to insinuate
himself into their instincts. He only half succeeds. Anders
and Fransine plan their rendezvous, but Anders, who has a
poet's acute eye for psychic abnormality, begins to suspect
whose idea it was.

Thus when Anders and Fransine meet at night at the
time and place determined by the councillor, who is spying
on them from his hiding place in the foliage, the scene
does not unfold as the latter had intended. In insulting and
hateful terms Anders rejects Fransine's love, until she
tremblingly asks: "Did you not want me to come, here, to
you, tonight?" "No," he replies, "if you are asking me my
honest opinion, Madame Fransine, no. I should like to be
by myself." Fransine turns away in despair and runs sob-
bing back toward her house. Anders sits quietly for a moment, then picks up his rifle. Turning around, he finds
himself standing face to face with the councillor—to the
amazement of the latter but not to Anders, who all the
while has felt the old man's clammy fingers around their
hearts. He fires his rifle into the body of the old man and
disappears from the garden.

The councillor falls to the ground mortally wounded, at
the same instant falling out of his godlike role. On his belly

he slowly crawls in the direction of Fransine's house. As he does, he tries to find consolation in the thought that he is under a greater spirit's, a great poet's, providential care. When finally, exhausted, bloody, and filthy, he reaches his fiancée he whispers: "Sacred, Fransine, we are sacred puppets"—at the same time moving his hand along the ground until it touches her foot. After a pause, he adds: "There the moon sits up high. You and I shall never die." "You!" cries Fransine. "You poet!" and shatters his head with a stone that she has torn loose from the garden wall. In this way these two newly created people fulfill what was written about the expulsion from paradise and about the enmity placed by God between the serpent and the woman: it shall bite her heel, but she shall crush its head.

In sum, the two tales that form the frame around the *Seven Gothic Tales* are about the marionette play from above and the marionette play from below, about God and the serpent, about the rules of life and damnation.

## 2. Winter's Tales

In *Out of Africa* Karen Blixen includes a little story that most people probably know in a slightly different form. She calls it "The Roads of Life" and tells it in such a way that, as if on a teeter-totter, a little joke is able to lift a heavy idea up into the light. The story, which ideally ought to be accompanied by a drawing, is about a man who lives in a little round house with a little round window in a little round garden. Nearby is a lake with lots of fish in it. One night the man is awakened by a dreadful noise. He gets up and goes out to investigate the sound. Awful things happen to him. He has the misfortune of falling over a stone twice and then into three ditches, one after the other. Eventually he discovers that the dam of the lake has broken; he repairs the break and returns home exhausted. If one follows the man's steps from the house to the lake and back again, one ends by having traced a very pretty picture of a stork. Blixen's commentary to this story begins as follows:

> I am glad that I have been told this story and I will remember it in the hour of need. The man in the story was cruelly deceived, and had obstacles put in his way. He must have thought: "What ups and downs! What a run of bad luck!" He must have wondered what was the idea of all his trials, he could not know that it was a story. But through them all he kept his purpose in view, nothing made him turn round and go home, he finished his course, he kept his faith. That man had his reward. In the morning he saw the stork. He must have laughed out loud then.
>
> The tight place, the dark pit in which I am now lying, of what bird is it the talon? When the design of my life is completed, shall I, shall other people see a stork? (Pp. 262–63)

The man in the story maintains his purpose; he keeps the idea of the author clear, as do the young lovers in "The Roads Round Pisa" who sacrifice all personal considerations for the passion implanted in them. He is one of the good marionettes, one of those whose reward is not comfort or any great degree of happiness but a destiny, a picture worth remembering. In his case it took the form of a stork.

Now if we were to consider that the author to whose plan the man in the story is so faithful has only a limited number of themes at his disposal, and that he alternates the successful ones, making use of the same pious formulas to fashion new destinies, we would see Blixen's marionettes in a new way: as figures enacting the limited number of valid destinies that are available down through the ages. This is how she expands the significance of the marionette symbol in *Winter's Tales*.

The structure of this collection of tales is strict and significant. There are eleven tales; the first (in the Danish version), "The Sailor Boy's Tale," announces the basic theme. The second and eleventh are tales about artists, and they frame the remaining eight. The first four of these give examples of how people with resolute and original natures are capable of liberating the courage in other people, of getting them to live up to their purpose and to step into a picture. Among these is "The Dreaming Child." The last four show lives that have become distorted and confused, small-scale reenactments of the Fall. "Alkmene" is one of these. "The Dreaming Child" and "Alkmene" are both about children who at the age of six are adopted into bourgeois families; in both cases their mere arrival is the stroke of the violin that causes certain musical figures to emerge.

In "The Dreaming Child" we are introduced to a prosperous shipowner's family that in the first half of the previous century inhabited one of the large houses along Bredegade. The present owners of both the firm and the house are the young couple Jacob and Emilie Vandamm. The wife, a woman with a flexible body and rigid morals, has married her husband for neither money nor love but because it was expected of her. She and Jacob are cousins and had been betrothed to each other since childhood. Shortly before their wedding, however, there was a moment when Emilie wanted to break the family agreement, because for the first time in her life she had fallen in love. The man was a young naval officer named Charley Dreyer. The night before departing on a long voyage he had proposed to Emilie that they spend the night together. Horrified, Emilie had fled from him, determined to uproot his image from her heart. A short time later she married Jacob, and a month after the wedding she learned that Charley had died of fever during his voyage. However, on the night Emilie left him, Charley had gone to another woman with the passion Emilie had awakened in his soul. The fruit of that encounter, a boy with a face like

Emilie's, has, upon the death of his mother, been placed
to grow up among strangers in an impoverished household
in Adelgade.*

The boy, Jens, feels like a stranger in this home, not
because of its poverty or because he knows anything about
his remarkable origin, but because he is a person whose
essence is dream and longing. For a while this longing becomes focused on the wealth of the great houses in Bredegade. An old seamstress, a woman who has spent her life
fantasizing about the opulence of the great houses, chooses
Jens as the heir to her unrealizable dreams. She tells him
that his feeling of being a stranger comes from the fact that
in reality he is the dearly loved child from one of the rich
houses who in some mysterious way has become separated
from his parents.

So when Emilie, whose marriage has been childless,
finally agrees with her husband, after careful reflection, to
adopt a child, and a providential chance selects Jens, the boy
is eminently well prepared for a solemn and heart-warming

---

*In a letter of August 9, 1952, sent to me by Karen Blixen upon the publication
of this essay, she wrote:

> I would like to point out one very simple disagreement between author
> and critic. I had not imagined the child Jens in "The Dreaming Child" as
> Charley Dreyer's son.
> Professor Brix asserts the contrary opinion in his book *Karen Blixens
> eventyr*, substantiating it up with various dates and facts which are not
> really in the story, and which, taken by themselves, seem somewhat con-
> fused. —For example, on p. 183, he states that Jacob marries Emilie in
> 1856, and that at that point she is 19 years old, and on p. 184, that the
> boy is born in 1850, the year when Charley left town for the West
> Indies—which means that Emilie, on the night Charley asks if he might
> spend the night with her, would have to have been 13 years old. He also
> says that Jacob and Emilie take Jens into their home approximately five
> years after their marriage, and then adds "at only six years of age, Jens
> is as precocious as a musical Wunderkind, life radiates within him, and
> he casts its glow all around him in the large lovely rooms and on the
> wealthy people of the capital." —which, in other words, does not fit with
> the stated date of Jens's birth either. But I did not want to get involved
> in pointing out small inaccuracies in the professor's analysis of "The
> Dreaming Child," since I already had to protest against a point at which
> he fundamentally misunderstood the plot of "Roads Round Pisa."
> Had I known that your lecture was to be published as a book by Wivel,
> I would have written to you earlier about this matter, also because your
> own justification of your view would have greatly interested me.

reunion. He does not enter the great house as a meek and miraculously elevated proletarian child but as a conqueror taking his duly appointed riches into possession. We should pay careful attention to the nature of his happiness. For him, his triumph does not consist in suddenly being able to dispose of all of the wonderful things around him but rather in the fact that his dreams have been fulfilled. The new things and the new people have only scant significance for him in and of themselves but enormous significance as signs that confirm his mighty visions.

"Jens took possession of the mansion in Bredegade," the narrator tell us, "and brought it to submission neither by might nor by power, but in the quality of that fascinating and irresistible personage, perhaps the most fascinating and irresistible in the whole world: the dreamer whose dreams come true." In this he reminds us of Joseph, who had much the same experience in the house of Potiphar and Pharaoh. The special quality of the magic emanating from Jens's person is that he brings the people around him to see themselves with dreamers' eyes and smilingly forces them to live up to an ideal. Jacob and Emilie become mild and powerful divinities, and even their stingy old kitchenmaid turns into the goddess of food and pots and pans, benefactress of mortals, a Ceres with an apron and a white ruff.

After a few months in his new house, Jens finds his longing moving in search of new areas, but without success. With increasing frequency his thoughts turn to his former, impoverished house. As he loses interest in his immediate surroundings, he falls ill, and a few months after his arrival in the wealthy house, he dies. Upon his death, the house in Bredegade collapses and reverts to what it was before, one house in a row of houses, and its inhabitants go back to their dull existences. Everyone except Emilie feels a great and painful loss. For her there had always been something upsetting about Jens's poetic temperament for which everything in life was equally good and which welcomed light and dark, joy and pain "in the same spirit of gallant, debonair approval and fellowship," for she had always struggled to distinguish between good and evil, right and wrong. Jens's attitude had disturbed her so profoundly that she had found it impossible to love him. Not until several months after his death has she absorbed his nature into her own and become transformed by it. In a conversation with Jacob she says, breaking a long silence: "He was my child, mine and Charley Dreyer's." She understands now that at the moment when, frightened and angry, she rejected her lover, she broke faith with a deeper and more essential passion than her passion for morality, and that somehow the destiny she betrayed incarnated itself in Jens's shining and fragile form. Emilie, who has always been so scrupulous in the cause of truth, begins to wish that she could believe that what has happened did not happen.

At one point in her conversation with Jacob, Emilie says, "I saw that we could not find another such as he, that there was none so wise." And then the narrator says: "She did not know that she was quoting from Scripture, any more than the old shipowner had been aware of doing so when he or-dained Jens to be buried in the field of his fathers and the cave that was therein." The verses of the Bible quoted here concern Joseph. After Joseph has interpreted the dream about the seven fat and the seven lean cattle, Pharaoh says of him, "None is so wise as he"; and the old shipowner's command refers to Joseph's bones being moved from Egypt to the burial place of Abraham's family in Canaan. Here it is clear that it is not only a question of a similarity between Joseph and Jens, a literary allusion, but of a kind of identity between their situations. If one pursues this line of thought a little further, one discovers a net of fine threads that connect the small figure of Jens to the legend of Joseph. Corresponding to Joseph's cosmic dream about the sun, moon, and eleven stars is Jens's great rainbow-colored dream, and the father whom Jens gets when he moves into the rich house is named Jacob, like Joseph's father, and like him, the latter Jacob is married to the daughter of his maternal uncle. However one interprets these connections, the intention behind them must be to show that Jens's story is a repetition in small format of Joseph's—that life, as it accomplishes the destiny of the strange little boy from Copenhagen, is in reality moving in old, well-known, and deeply engrained traces.

In the second story, "Alkmene," a Jutland pastor and his wife who have no children adopt a six-year-old girl, Alkmene. The child's origins are obscure, but it is nevertheless clear that a mixture of noble and artists' blood flows in her veins. Alkmene is a strange child; she has a glow of happiness and joie de vivre about her. She startles and upsets with her nonchalantly self-assured behavior and with her strange mixture of virtues and failings. She balances fearlessly on the roof ridge of the house, she gives away her new clothes, and she takes whatever anyone says to her to be literally true. She loves music and dancing, and the bright glow that surrounds her when she dances shows that dancing is part of her essential nature. She trembles and grows pale at the sight of a dead bird, but she pulls grass snakes from the hedges and carries them around without flinching. It is easier to state the qualities Alkmene lacks than the ones she has; she lacks the qualities humanity acquired through the Fall: fear, knowledge of good and evil and of the necessity of death, hatred of the snake. This remarkably wild and enchanting child grows up in a Jutland parsonage permeated by the heavy spirit of bourgeois Christianity, and she is cared for by a couple whose view of life is rooted in the Fall. By "the Fall" I mean the doubling of the self or its splitting, the mental act whereby human beings step outside of themselves and, after seeing that they are naked, perceive physical nature as a mystery that arouses both anxiety and desire. The Fall is the moment that brings both sin and virtue, both the Satan of instinct and the God of duty, into existence.

Alkmene's stepmother, the pastor's wife, Gertrud, is a warm and motherly woman, hard-working and energetic, dutifully laboring under the curse uttered when mankind was driven out of paradise. She loves Alkmene with a great, demanding, possessive love. She loves her and wants to own her, dress her up, hug her, but Alkmene is shy of being touched. She is fond of her stepmother at the start but cannot reciprocate her kind of love, which eventually becomes a torture for her. Twice, once when she is nine and again when she is eleven, she tries to run away, but both times she is brought back. "Why did you run away? Why did you want to leave us?" Gertrud asks her over and over. It is also Gertrud who tries to teach Alkmene to feel fear and who, without a word of reproach, with dutiful conscientiousness, sits at home darning Alkmene's stockings when the girl comes home from a bright and carefree day. Gradually the wish to free herself from Gertrud at any cost takes shape in Alkmene's soul.

Alkmene's stepfather, Pastor Jens Jespersen, has a deeper, more fearful understanding of the special quality of the child he has taken into his house. He, too, has had a problematical past. As a young theology student he suffered a spiritual crisis, brought on by his reading about the Greek world with its gods and nature spirits, its theater and art, its glorious vision of nature. All of this represented a threat to his soul, for he saw nature as sinful. It is a well-known law that one cannot indulge in what one considers to be sinful without truly sinning. In his fantasy, therefore, as he turned away from the world of ancient Greece, he began to see himself as someone chosen by God for a great role in life, perhaps as a leader, a man of destiny. On the verge of falling victim to megalomania, he fled from Copenhagen and took refuge in a sense of duty and stern, renunciatory piety— still tempted by the glow emanating from nature and genius and forever on guard against it. Thus he allows no dancing at the parsonage—while it is precisely in dancing that Alkmene gives expression to her true essence. He begins to instruct her in the classics, and Alkmene drinks in classical learning with desire and energy; but her joy makes him suspicious and he cuts short her instruction. Thus each of her talents is met in the parsonage by an interdiction.

When Alkmene turns fifteen she receives a large inheritance, presumably from her unknown father. It makes no impression on her but a great one on her stepfather. The prospect of so much money fills him with nervous agitation.

"But if it is to be, here, a trial of strength between God and Mammon, should I decline to take on the championship of the Lord?" "Indeed," he adds, "I have known from the first that through Alkmene some great task might come to me. And when I am dead, I shall live on in her good works." A short time later he dies, and thus death comes into Alkmene's house and into her heart. She understands that this was what she had wished for her stepmother.

A few months later Alkmene asks her friend Vilhelm to accompany her in secret to Copenhagen. Once they arrive in town, she tells him that she has come for the purpose of observing a public execution. "No," she replies to Vilhelm's shocked objections, "it is not an entertainment. It is a warning to the people who may be near to doing the same thing themselves, and who will be warned by nothing else." Then she quotes a saying of her stepfather's: "For God alone knows all. And who can say of himself: Of this deed I could never have been guilty?" Alkmene shivers and trembles as she stands at the foot of the scaffold, and when the executioner's axe falls she nearly faints. This is Alkmene's Fall from grace. The pressure on her has built to the point where at last it has robbed her of her effortless balance of nature and instinct that had been her innocence and strength. The pastor's death had made her look with fear into her own heart. And in her confusion Alkmene found it necessary to impress upon herself the old teaching, that the wages of sin are death. Later in her life the pastor's prediction of living on in Alkmene's deeds is fulfilled. She avoids anything capable of arousing pleasure or desire and gives herself over to the permissible vice of serving Mammon. In sterility and stinginess she lives her life, falling deeper than other people because she fell fully and entirely.

A remarkable aspect of Alkmene's story is that the person who tells it, her friend Vilhelm, does not really understand it. Her life contained a mighty promise, yet it became empty and desolate. And Vilhelm's own life became impoverished and colorless once Alkmene slipped out of it. But he does not see that he was the cause of the break in Alkmene's fate—that both of their lives were robbed of their meaning because he and the pastor, the two people closest to her, were so alienated from their instincts that they had only the vaguest and dreamiest suspicion of their real purpose in life. The reader, however, can see that this is the case, thanks to the mythical traits, though half erased and almost unrecognizable, that keep appearing in their story. They hint at an ancient pattern of destiny that one can find perhaps in its clearest and most valid form in the myth of Alkmene of Thebes.

The Greek woman Alkmene was married to the soldier Amphitryon; Zeus fell in love with her, but to obtain a night in the arms of this faithful wife the god had to take on her husband's form. Afterward, when Alkmene learns who has visited her bed and whom she has mistakenly experienced with all her heart and all of her senses as Amphitryon, she falls into such a painful state of doubt about her own nature and instincts that it threatens to undo her. But she remains true to her earthly lover/husband and comes through her trial alive and intact. That is why she is able to give birth to Zeus's son, Heracles, the great slayer of monsters. The first time the pastor and Vilhelm hear Alkmene's name, the former quotes a remark of Zeus's: "Who bore me Heracles, a child staunch of heart." And Vilhelm dreams of her at night: "She met me on a path in the field, in the midst of the tall wheat, and the capital A in her name shone like silver." The shining *A* does not signify only Alkmene, as Vilhelm thinks, but also Amphitryon. In the myth we are told that Amphitryon, on the way home from war, wanted to send his wife a diadem with his name on it. Zeus beat him to it and sent an identical diadem but with the first letter of his name on it. Later the husband's diadem played an important role in clearing up the nocturnal intrigue, for it was with his *A* that Alkmene demonstrated her irreproachable fidelity. Vilhelm often has a dream in which Alkmene disappears and he, in great anxiety and despair, goes looking for her, but during the day it does not occur to him that he actually could lose her. At the root of his being, in other words, he has preserved a reminiscence of his true identity, as the pastor also has with his megalomaniac fantasies, but both men lack the requisite simplicity and instinctiveness to live their roles as Amphitryon and Zeus. Instead, they betray Alkmene and her demands on them—they drag her down and disrupt the harmony of her being. Thus it is only in a caricatural and crippled form that she can fulfill her destiny.

In this discussion I have tried to give an idea of the plots and the coherence of these two *Winter's Tales*. For my conclusion I will attempt to shed some light on the motif of repetition that plays such an important and remarkable role in them. I will refer to an essay by Thomas Mann, which was originally written in honor of Freud's eightieth birthday. It is entitled "Freud and the Future," and is in fact a commentary on Mann's own series of Joseph novels. There is good reason to think that Karen Blixen took a different and more personal road to her theme, so I do not know if she would have accepted the extension of perspective that I am about to propose to her story.

Thomas Mann introduces the main thesis of his essay by comparing Freud's distinction between the regulating, form-giving agency of the mind, the ego, and the blind, protoplasmic force, the id, with Schopenhauer's distinction between intellect and will. Then he takes the reader into a discussion of Schopenhauer's notion of the apparent purposefulness in the destiny of individuals. In brief, he suggests that in the same way as our nocturnal dreams are formed by our will, without our awareness or conscious control, so is reality a greater dream dreamed by the ur-will in all of us. After having thus enlarged the scope of the discussion, Mann turns back to psychoanalysis to discuss an essay by an Austrian analyst. It concerns the way in which artists' biographies used to be written. The very predictable and schematic nature of these books suggests that their primary intention was to show that the life in question had unfolded according to the proper formula, that it had followed an immemorial and hence legitimate pattern. He states that in many cases it is impossible to say what is legend, what is formula, and what is specific to the life of the individual artist. This can also be the case with modern people. Not only artists' lives but every life is determined by conscious and unconscious acts of identification. We all live the life of a certain category, of a certain profession or class.

Mann ends the essay with a description of the Joseph novels. He writes that it is correct to place his work in the boundary area between the typical and the individual, and it is appropriate to apply the viewpoint of psychoanalysis to it. As an author, he says, he has moved from the depiction of the bourgeois/individual life to the mythical/typical one. When psychology moves from the individual to the type, it enters the area of myth. The typical and the mythical are the same. And the reenactment of myth is the ordering idea of the Joseph novels. He goes on to explain that with *depth psychology*, another term often used for psychoanalysis, *depth* is to be understood also in a chronological sense. To penetrate into the soul of a present-day child is at the same time to penetrate into the primitive, into the childhood of the race. Primeval time is the well where the archetypes of all the myths—the norms of life—are to be found. This is where the timeless paradigms of human life take shape that each life unconsciously reproduces as it fashions its own characteristics. Thomas Mann finds great happiness in this insight, a bright cheerfulness, *Heiterkeit*. He calls it the smiling awareness of the eternal, of the being that lasts forever, of the paradigm to which life conforms and by which it achieves validity as a repetition of eternal truths, of humanity's footsteps in deeply worn tracks. And by taking examples from history he shows how at the moment of death, the most personal moment for each of them, the great figures of antiquity triumphantly seized upon a quotation to show that finally they had consummated a life in the form of myth. Thus, of Christ's words on the cross, "My God, my God, why hast Thou forsaken me?" he says that despite their notes of despair and disappointment they are the expression of the highest degree of messianic self-awareness. For these words are not original; they are not a spontaneous outcry, but a quotation—from the Twenty-second Psalm, which from beginning to end is a prophesy about the Messiah. And the quotation means: I am the one who was awaited, I am the Messiah who lived and died as it was written. Thus out of despair and individual misery and defeat rise an unconquerable optimism and mood of mythical rejoicing.

At the conclusion of his essay he brings the entire chain of his thoughts to rest in a symbol, the marionette comedy, the Punch and Judy show in which puppets perform a fixed and familiar set of actions. As just such a theatrical fulfillment of a predetermined plot does life appear when seen in the artistic optic of myth. The premise of the Joseph novels is the moment of insight when the individual becomes aware that he is a kind of marionette character. The happiness and equanimity felt by Joseph in the novel comes from an awareness deep inside of himself that he holds the main part in an old play, that he is identical to the Egyptian god who was torn to pieces, buried, and then lifted up again. Both the misery and the triumph in his destiny are equally essential for the beauty and harmony of the play.

As for applying these theories to Karen Blixen's writing, it is appropriate to point out that Thomas Mann had achieved an artist's insight into this combined repetition and mask motif long before he had intellectually acquired the theory to support it.

Earlier I referred to Heinrich von Kleist's *On the Marionette Comedy*. The dialog ends with the witty and profound statement that only marionettes and God have absolute gracefulness, since both are beings that consist of either absolute nature or pure spirit. In a Danish context we might say that repetition is experienced only by a marionette or a Christian, and at the mention of the latter our thoughts turn to Søren Kierkegaard, author of a book entitled *Repetition*. In this concept it is possible for Søren Kierkegaard and Karen Blixen to meet, moved by the same fear of the demonic aesthete, but they meet only to move in opposite directions away from this figure and to pursue two very different forms of piety.

# The Messenger

When I first began to visit Karen Blixen in her home, I would occasionally feel like saying: "Why not let's just relax?" But I never said it, and I never did relax, because there was not that kind of easiness about her. She had brightness and fire and distant promises in her, and deadly boredom, complaints, and contempt, but in both her strength and weakness she was wide awake, as dry and resonant as a crystal.

As she was when I met her eleven years ago, so must she have been, more or less, in all the years during which she was an author in Denmark. She had survived the hopes and proclivities that for most people constitute life, without in the process becoming reconciled with herself. Her passions had branched off into other, previously unforeseen areas, and she was now living, visibly and publicly, in regions to which otherwise only dreams give access. That was why she had such an unspeakable power to remind me of something—of forgotten promises or dangers or oversights. At the start, my relationship with Karen Blixen was an un-

interrupted déjà vu experience, one often painfully height-
ened to the point of complete confusion.

This feeling was not mutual nor, of course, constant, for
after emotional uproar come exhaustion and reflection. It
was Karen Blixen's fate in her later years to make her way
unchanged through spiritual friendships that evolved along
curves like violent passions, abruptly rising and falling, and
that altered the life of the other person.

As a matter of course and, in the beginning, unnotice-
ably, the boundaries between my inner and outer world became fluid in her company, for she bore down on me from
both sides. What previously had been the ground of my consciousness began to move under her influence and to give
rise to forms and faces. Longings and possibilities that I had
not felt before began to rise inside and grope their way
forward. She had the power to conjure such feelings when
she opened herself to me. But for the most part her approach
was an external and a different one; she wanted to be nour-
ished and amused, or if not that then at least recognized as
who she was, as someone untouchably distant in terms of
reputation and rank and age. And if that, too, was not possible, then at least she wanted me to admit that she was the
most solitary of people, that in all of Denmark she had not
one friend who would lift a finger for her. And when she had
given voice to hours' worth of complaint, and when I had
given up hope and at last was about to leave, then she could
say in tones of sorrow: "To a person like me one must show
limitless forbearance."

She touched my heart like an irreparable sorrow. She
could seem so utterly abandoned. But she had no tolerance
for pity and met its approach as blankly and coldly as sheer
glass or unbroken wall. No matter how quick and understanding I tried to be, my efforts never amounted to more
than touching bagatelles—"How sweet of you"—and were
instantly consumed in the great flame of her. Under no circumstances was she willing to return to propriety and bourgeois virtue. Positioned between her hunger for people and

her rejection of the modest nourishment I was able to provide, it was easy to lose my balance, for she could be intoxicating, too, and in her company I became interesting to myself. Then I could be misled into wanting to reach her at the place where, in the plain sight of everyone, she was, and at that instant the situation became hopelessly skewed and I ran head-on into inevitable defeats. During the years when I came to her home at Rungstedlund I had more than one occasion to think brotherly thoughts about Shakespeare's Malvolio and his dreadful mistake.

I did make mistakes, but I made them with a force and a scope that I had never before attempted. At the start I was perhaps solely responsible for my mistakes, but later on, when the situation was more complicated, she would assist with the appropriate stories. Through bitter personal experience Karen Blixen was profoundly familiar with a certain line in human life that separates our dreams, passions, and weaknesses from our consciousness of what other people think of us. *Line* is not a strong term, but the reality of it was. Under no circumstances did I want to have strangers in certain areas, but suddenly there she was. She was utterly familiar with what it meant to be a human being; she was aware of the unmapped longings that she provoked at the point when they were still almost dormant and just starting to drift out into the ordinary light of day. At the right moment, which she could unfailingly determine, she would wake the sleepwalker and call his attention to his pajamas and to the state of his hair. At the instant when you realize that everyone is looking at you in your disarray, a great deal of greenness can get burned away and many tender threads broken. But upon that same threshold you can also learn the art of losing face and letting it lie, for the boundary line between the inner and the outer world is also the place where citizenship in both worlds can be acquired.

I made mistakes, but I did so because there was reality in my relationship to Karen Blixen, and not only in the way and in the context that I had first imagined. I still had good reasons to be grateful to her, but they were different ones.

Fantasies, illusions, large golden mirror reflections that gave rise to mistaken longings—these were Karen Blixen's gifts to her friends. And gifts they were, great shining fruits that were bitter on the tongue but full of nourishment. It is this kind of generosity that Sophus Claussen yearningly evokes in his poem *Midsummer* when he exclaims:

> *The good angels all have fallen*
> *and are no more.*
> *Has Fairytale a coal black angel*
> *by chance in store?*

For in the area of illusion two roads always lie open, and that is why savior and seducer are often difficult to distinguish from each other and can at times be one and the same person. The one road leads in passion's familiar direction out toward honor and wealth, and the other runs against the stream back toward the source, the reverse and inward road of insight into the passions that are the source of error.

The kinds of personal experiences I had with Karen Blixen reopened my eyes to her writings and aided my understanding of the enchanting and repellent ambiguity of her unique oeuvre. Its character of mirage, of religious phantasmagoria, suddenly became clear. Just as an excellent parody can transmit the inspiration of a lost original, so in Karen Blixen's tales are people's highest divine possibilities preserved in the mode of mirror reflection and caricature within the world of sensual passion. This is why enthusiasm and fear run confusingly together in the reader as he moves through the lunar landscape of her tales.

In a time like the present, when the inner strength of the human being is waning while his external power is increasing, it is a joy to have known a person like Karen Blixen, who had the power and the means to go through another person's bones and marrow and to open up his inner world of dangers and unslayable hope. I could be afraid of her, but I could not be bitter toward her or regret any part of my relationship with her. For that she bore too strong a mark of necessity. And despite all her weaknesses she was a great and strong person, thoroughly schooled in pain and as implacable as a ritual, both to herself and to others. It was like meeting the seductress of legend, the wild and ruthlessly devoted Kundry. And like Kundry, she brought in her life and art the only kind of message about the Holy Grail that is still within the power of an overly clever and desperate age to assimilate.

To be recognized in her specificity and ambiguity was crucial for her. She constantly took pains to be seen as a person who lived outside the current norms and system of values. To the public she passionately insisted on the note of privilege in her fate and resolutely played a great and demanding role, ever mindful of its potentially comical sides. But to a narrower circle she just as frequently presented herself as humiliated and rejected, as a disenfranchised person outside the law, living a life about whose perils she had to warn her friends. In this regard she would use words and expressions pointless to repeat here, because they are no longer fashionable and would give the wrong impression. But in her later years she would let fall veil after veil and, in her way, lay bare her peculiar nature. One example can show what I mean.

Most conversations that I had with Karen Blixen that were not concerned with the most immediate and harmless topics were drawn from her repertory, the four- to five-hour-long lesson, which anyone can reconstitute by putting together her final twenty-five years of interviews, then subtracting the repetitions. When I first knew her she rarely ventured outside of this area, but when she would occasionally gather her attention and focus it directly on me, she would always accompany the event with a little, surprising ceremony. She would take off her kerchief or shawl and draw it over her mouth and lower face, and would speak and listen to me in this disguise. This was not more surprising than many other things, and I found no occasion to ask her the reason for it. One evening several years later, at a time of

great adversity for me, she asked me to tell her about
myself—in fact she pressured me to do so in the strongest
way. And so I began to talk; but then, looking up, I lost the
thread of what I was saying, for in the semidarkness of the
green living room the lower half of her face was shining like
a silver plate being held up to the light. And again several
years after that, she published a picture of herself on the
cover of her book *Shadows on the Grass* in which she is shown
standing on one leg and with the light falling on the lower
part of her face, thus visually relating herself to the dangerous, utterly powerful women in her tales.

# CHAPTER 3

# Karen Blixen's Place in Modern European Literature

The real reason I stand here tonight delivering a lecture about Karen Blixen is that I have long felt that I owed Frans Lasson, the chairman of the Karen Blixen Society, an answer. On several occasions he has asked me to contribute to the series of memoirs he originated that could bear the collective title "My Relationship with Karen Blixen" and to which Thorkild Bjørnvig, Clara Svendsen, Thomas Dinesen, and Caroline Carlsen have contributed. Each time, upon reflection, I have declined, not because I lacked inclination but for reasons that I could not ignore. My lecture this evening is a kind of explanation of this refusal. As to its title, I might perhaps say that in the conclusion I actually will get to the announced topic, Karen Blixen's place in European literature, though only so far as to locate her in that context. I hope this will meet with your satisfaction.

If I were to begin with my answer, that is, the reason expressed in its simplest terms for my not writing a book of memoirs, I would have to say: Because there is no language adequate to the relationship I had with her. I do not mean that Danish lacks words that could describe it, but by language I mean something more specific than arbitrary combinations of words. I mean that I could not describe it by using the linguistic conventions that we routinely observe, or in any case observe when speaking of our ordinary affairs. A common feature of the memoirs mentioned above is that the conventional attitudes of their respective authors nullify the truly radical qualities of Karen Blixen.

Before going on, I want to say just a few more words about my personal relationship with her. I happened to meet Karen Blixen because she liked some essays I had published about her. She initiated our acquaintanceship. Knowing her personally gave her books a dimension for me that they scarcely would have had otherwise. In the final analysis my view of her—as hers was of Byron, that is, that his real masterpiece was his life—is that her life is greater than her books; it adds up to a larger, a more astounding, and a far more desperate unity than her books. They have an air of great serenity, as if written by a person of easy self-confidence. That was hardly the case with her.

If I were to place Karen Blixen in the world of substances, to use the language of chemistry, I might say that she belonged among the euphoric ones. In more familiar terms, I would call her a critical spirit, critical in the sense that she was never satisfied with her current situation. She found it lacking. She had an inspiring way of criticizing it so that she created expectations and hopes for the future. She always found some element in her present situation—inadequate, no doubt, in itself—that could be developed so that far in the dim future it would become what one most desired. Her attitude, in other words, was double: on the one hand it contained inspiration, expectation, and promise, and on the other, the fierce reproach that was their inseparable obverse.

Not only did she find her current situation lacking, she felt the same about the people around her. She wanted to take them apart and then put them back together in a newer and better way, and if that were not possible, then onto the scrap heap with them. Along with her promises came reproaches, and along with the reproaches entire landscapes of complaint and lamentation, an inexhaustible supply. There is a good deal of truth in what Ole Wivel has written about me, that in time this incessant source of complaint in Karen Blixen became a greater mystery to me than the prospects she opened.

After a while, her reproaches added a dimension to the way I read her. In an old book (*Wilhelm Meister*) Goethe writes of a young man who, on his way through life, has a relationship with a famous and brilliant actress named Aurelia. An embodied metaphor, she carries a sharp, pointed knife that she often unsheathes and waves around menacingly. She is like Irene in Ibsen's *When We Dead Awaken*, who is similarly equipped with both a knife and a needle, constantly threatening to kill any man who comes close to her. Goethe shows what these weapons mean in a passage where Aurelia, who is raging against her companion, men in general, and the theater public, is finally interrupted by the young man, who asks her: "My friend, are you unable to stop sharpening the dagger with which you are constantly hurting yourself?" This shows that her dagger and her invective are equivalent and analogous. About the young man listening to the complaints, Goethe writes: "His friend's frightful condition, half spontaneous and half forced, tormented him. Inside he felt the pain of her dreadful agitation. His brain became disturbed and his blood began to move feverishly."

Here we are no longer dealing with the kind of reproaches familiar to us from our everyday bourgeois households. Here reproach has become criticism and criticism has become a kind of art form, a tool, a destructive radiation. The person at whom it was directed felt that his armor, his protective shield, was being broken down, and he felt as if he were being swept into a sphere of experience previously closed to him, one that perhaps he would have wished to ignore but that now, because of this process, had been opened. One may wonder what sort of things provoked her criticism. They were, of course, any unfortunate personal qualities that her interlocutor happened to have, but they were also any disadvantages he had simply by belonging to the male sex, or to the Danish people. That is, her accusations were of a scope that made it impossible to take them personally.

Yet out of all this came a rapport: I was one-half of a relationship in which destructive radiation emanated from the other half. This left me with two choices: either to go my way or to try to make use of the process—to sort through her stream of complaints and establish a kind of balance with her—though I never really felt our relationship was natural or equal. There were many reasons why it was not. Nevertheless, I was the one who finally had to say: Either we establish a balance, a kind of equality between us, or we are through. I was forced into the position of having to try to determine the moment when the situation veered over and slipped out of both her and my control. On that score her writings were enormously helpful, first of all because in them things happen under her conscious control to a much greater degree than in life, but also—and with this I will end my personal reminiscences—because when Karen Blixen criticized, she also intervened in your life. She created situations that produced surprising effects, surprising in the sense that they showed that she had knowledge about you that, from a naturalistic standpoint, ought to have been totally inaccessible. Beneath the surface of our violently agitated scenes something else was taking place that called for an expertise far beyond anything I had previously experienced.

If this process had been something that just took place between the two of us, I would not have been able to profit from it. If I had known only her writings, I would not have seen it. But the combination sharpened my attention to depths in her writings that gradually became clearer, and it led me into areas that, to use a ready-made phrase, I might say were concerned with analyses of the decision-making process. *Decision-making process* is a phrase that occurs so often in modern journalistic language that perhaps I should specify what I mean by it: Karen Blixen's readers often feel

that it is easy to enter into the milieu of her tales; it is easy
to grasp the characters. Unlike some modern novels and
short stories that are hard to enter, her stories seem inviting
and clearly defined. On the other hand, it can be difficult to
understand why any given story ends as it does and what
in fact has happened along the way. This is because crucial
things happen in her stories on a level where one is not
accustomed to look for them.

If one were to pose the following questions to Karen
Blixen's tales—and now I am focusing on her central collection of stories, *Winter's Tales*, a profound book that is also
her most open and instructive one—"At what moment is an
action decided? What decisions are made? When does a character personally decide to perform an action that then becomes the decisive factor in the plot?" one finds her texts
responding at depths where, earlier, I would not have thought
it possible to formulate thoughts and to make observations.

A contemporary British author, Iris Murdoch, who in
essential ways is similar to Karen Blixen, or who knows some
of the things that Karen Blixen knew—perhaps we should
put it the other way around and say that distinct traces of
some of the things Karen Blixen knew can also be found in
Iris Murdoch—in one of her later novels, *The Black Prince*,
performs the kind of analysis I mean. The passage is divided
into two parts; the first part deals with the production of
art, the second part with moral decisions:

> In the light of later events I was disposed to regard almost
> everything I did during the period so far narrated as
> blameworthy. I dare say human wickedness is sometimes
> the product of a sort of conscious leeringly evil intent. . . .
> But more usually it is the product of a semi-deliberate
> inattention, a sort of swooning relationship to time. As I
> said in the beginning, any artist knows that the space be-
> tween the stage where the work is too unformed to have
> committed itself and the stage where it is too late to im-
> prove it can be as thin as a needle. Genius perhaps consists
> in opening out this needle-like area until it covers almost

the whole of the working time. Most artists, through sheer idleness, weariness, inability to attend, drift again and again and again from the one stage straight into the other, in spite of good resolutions and the hope with which each new work begins. This is of course a moral problem, since all art is the struggle to be, in a particular sort of way, virtuous. There is an analogous transition in the everyday proceedings of the moral agent. We ignore what we are doing until it is too late to alter it. We never allow ourselves quite to focus upon moments of decision; and these are often in fact hard to find even if we are searching for them. We allow the vague pleasure-seeking annoyance-avoiding tide of our being to hurry us onward until the moment when we announce that we can no other. There is thus an eternal discrepancy; between the self-knowledge which we gain by observing ourselves objectively and the self-awareness which we have of ourselves subjectively: a discrepancy which probably makes it impossible to arrive at the truth. Our self-knowledge is too abstract, our self-awareness is too intimate and swoony and dazed. Perhaps some kind of integrity of the imagination, a sort of moral genius, could verify the scene, producing minute sensibility and control of the moment as a function of some much larger consciousness. Can there be a *natural*, as it were Shakespearean, felicity in the moral life? Or are Eastern sages right to set as a task to their disciples the gradual total destruction of the dreaming ego? (Pp. 156–57)

Karen Blixen had this kind of discerning, stalking, indeed hunting moral genius, which was not, to be honest, what I expected to find when I first met her. I imagined that I was about to enter a universe similar to her books, a universe where people were allowed to be who they were and where the moral conventions that had so complicated my life up until now were nonexistent. That was a grave mistake. She had a unique kind of intellectual strength for pursuing people into the place of their innermost decisions and for sensing the atmosphere around these decisions—a strength that she directed outward and not, as I have already indicated, back upon herself with anything like the same rigor.

From one of Karen Blixen's fairy tales, "The Fish," I will give you an example of a moment filled with an acute, analytical awareness of the process involved in a moment of decision. The process remains obscure for the character making the decision and in the story it is never subsequently explained, but it is clear that the narrator understands it. I will summarize just enough of the story to make my point.

At a certain point in the story, King Erik—that is, Erik Glipping—is traveling with a friend from his youth, Sune Pedersen, who has just returned from Paris. They are riding on horseback down to the seashore outside Søborg in North Sealand. The king is on his way to visit Granze, his father's old Wendish thrall, a sorcerer with whom he spent much time in his childhood. When the two noble riders reach the downs and Granze sees them, he walks toward them, but he directs his greeting exclusively to Sune, with the words: "Is it you who have come here, Sune, kinsman of Absalon?" A little later, when they are sitting around Granze's fire, he says to the king: "Now I shall tell you why I was afraid to speak to you when I first saw you. As you came over the downs you had a shining ring round your head, such as your holy pictures have. Where did you get that?" No answer is given, and the only one who could have given it is Granze himself, as becomes evident in the following passage. Note the use of the past tense as they sit by the fire: "As you came riding, you had a shining ring around your head; I was afraid to speak to you." But now they are sitting and talking together without fear. Why is that? Because the king no longer has the ring. Thus one might say that the real focus of the story is the movements of a ring from place to place and the various forms in which it manifests itself.

As for the king, this is the day after a strange, sleepless night during which he reviewed his situation and recognized that he was sick and tired of fighting with his vassals, sick and tired at the thought of the many women who have lain in his arms. His powerful egoism prevents him from finding his equal among mortal human beings, and so, as his thoughts take a heavenly turn, he ends by imagining himself as the rival, so to speak, of the king of heaven. He would gallantly wear the glove of the Virgin Mary on his helmet, he thinks, as his reverie moves in an adoring, dimly sexual direction. What Karen Blixen is addressing here is a central theme not only in her own writings, but one that is omnipresent in nineteenth-century bourgeois literature—that is, the way in which sexual desire, passion, whenever it is blocked, acts like a dammed-up stream and moves from its natural location up into the head. Much of literature concerns itself with this phenomenon, from the troubador poetry of the twelfth century up to approximately World War I, when the theme begins to die out. Much of the poet Grundtvig's youth was concerned with tracing the alternate paths in which blocked desire moves. Each time a new pathway was opened inside him he experienced an abrupt expansion of knowledge, so that in his case one literally can speak of a tree of knowledge. And if this process played a significant part in Grundtvig's youth, it provided the entire logic of Sophus Claussen's authorship. Someplace in his writing Claussen remarks that nothing which exists disappears, but if it is repressed, it will reappear in an unexpected form. And if one has not seen this unexpected form anywhere else, one can see it in some of the paintings Willumsen painted in his youth; in several self-portraits there is around his head a shining ring of the kind we are talking about.

On their ride to the coast, Sune has not revealed, nor has he been entirely able to keep secret, the sweet and secret love he is feeling. He has just returned from Paris, where —within the limits of his priestly vow of chastity—he has experienced a romantic, melting, languishing, and adoring love for a noble lady. He is still full of soft and airy feelings that tie him to Paris, and his memories of Paris begin to merge with his notion of paradise. When Granze meets him, he not only greets him in the way I quoted earlier—"Is it you who have come here, Sune, kinsman of Absalon?"—but right after that he says: "I thought you were dead." "Nay, not dead yet, by the grace of God," says Sune, smiling. "You came near to it, though, seven full moons ago," says Granze. "Yes, that is so," says Sune gravely. But then Granze chuckles and says: "A woman cooked a nice dish for you, and put ratsbane in it. Did she take you for a rat, little Sune? If the rats would go into the holes God made for them, people would not poison them." Sune had grown pale. He sat on his horse without a word.

What is taking place at this moment is something that Sune later compares to Granze's disembowelment of the newly caught fish: Sune's romantic, adoring love is being ripped out of him, his priestly virtue mocked and his most precious secret thrown down onto the sand. But of course at the same time—and Granze knows this—the king's secret is also being exposed. Granze cleverly aims his weapon at Sune and does indeed strike him, but the person he is really aiming at is the king, and so it follows that this is the moment when the ring, which the king previously had around his head, disappears—only to reappear a few minutes later, when Granze pulls it as a metal ring out of the fish he has just caught and cleaned. The ring has moved from the head down into the fish, which here clearly functions as a sex symbol.

This short scene reveals a number of things, the first of which is a knowledge of the erotic and the many ways in which it manifests itself—a knowledge that is not so widespread now as it was in former times, despite the obvious fact that today the energy paths of repressed eroticism support an entire industry: the pornography business. The business is built on the premise that a person can look at a picture and have a relationship with a person who is not physically present, but the relationship is nonetheless real in the sense that it brings about a significant change in the spectator's organism. These are utterly familiar facts, of course, yet at the same time they are also quite remarkable.

This particular aspect of sexuality, so central to Karen Blixen's work, which is deeply rooted in it both as a potentiality and as a process, forms the background to the plot. The second thing revealed by this scene is a knowledge of when things happen. The third thing is an awareness of the sort of power that would be required to deflect the king's intentions in a new direction. It turns out that ridicule would do it, the sight of Sune as he is made a laughingstock and his love mocked and shown to be a thin, airy infatuation. At that moment occurs the decisive action in the tale: events shift and the king takes a new tack. He is not aware of this himself; but Granze, wielding his knife, has with one stroke traced the course of the remaining events.

A similar analysis could be made of each of Blixen's *Winter's Tales*, that is, an analysis that would reach down and grasp these psychic processes—psychic/organic, one might call them, little-known psychosomatic processes—but this analysis would also reveal, precisely because the processes are unconscious or only half conscious, the extent to which they are controlled by events in the outside world.

There are some additional aspects of these tales I would like to mention. The first, a profoundly characteristic one, is that these tales, which are known to be concerned with the pathways of fate—something that sounds grand and exciting and ethereal and seems to invite all kinds of metaphysical speculation—when they themselves explore these paths, they trace them to their point of origin, that is, to a place that turns out not to be metaphysical in the usual sense of the term. Instead, the paths originate at a level of consciousness to which human beings ordinarily have no access. And even after one has come to see that knowledge of these things is present in her stories, one also realizes that it is not there as a readily available gift. The knowledge at the core of her work is essentially veiled by symbolic language.

Furthermore, one can say of her analyses that they are almost always focused on one specific constellation, namely, the relationship between sex and consciousness. The sexual relation in Karen Blixen's writings is always viewed in two ways: on the one hand, with critical indignation on behalf of women for the numerous injustices perpetrated on them by men—this we can call the moral view; good use could be made of it in certain types of contemporary feminist analysis.

Running contrary to the current of moral indignation, on the other hand, is one that persists, almost to an inconceivable degree, in seeing the relationship between man and woman as a passion. In this, Karen Blixen goes almost as far—in fact she does go as far—as to see the most sacred of relationships from the religious texts upon which she draws so heavily as suffused with earthly passion. Take, for example, from her book of posthumous writings, *Carnival*, the last tale, "Second Meeting." It is about a meeting between Byron and an Italian puppet theater director. In it we are told that what happened to Mary, the mother of Jesus, during the miracle of Pentecost and the descent of the Holy Spirit, was a reawakening of her memory of the passionate union that she experienced thirty-four years previously and is presently reliving. Karen Blixen's insistence on the religious element in her portrayal of the world of passion is as consistent a current as the feminist one.

Another particular and extremely important characteristic of Karen Blixen's writings—as became apparent in our reading of "The Fish"—is this: that when crucial decisions are made, they stem from a sphere or zone of activity that one can say is located on the border between consciousness and the organism. One example, as we saw, is the shining ring that appears and disappears around the king's head, a process that the text, read in a certain way, describes. Or the fire in the opera house in "The Dreamers," which of course is not merely a fire in a theater building but a fire in the blood that builds to a point where it attacks Pellegrina's body. It is inevitable in these stories that the things that belong to the world of conscious decision first manifest themselves in another form, a provisional physical form. I will say more about this later; for the moment let me simply say that this remarkable in-between space forms a kind of line, or limit, through all of her writings.

Before I try to analyze this phenomenon, let me give one more example from the story "Copenhagen Season," from which, as before, I will take an incident without interpreting the whole story. It is about a love affair between two young people that was said—presumably by Karen Blixen—to be modeled on a supposed relationship between her father and Agnes Frijs. Whether this is true or not, I do not know, nor does it matter. It concerns a relationship between two young people at the close of the nineteenth century who, as they used to say, both belong to the upper level of society, but do so in a way that still leaves an enormous distance between them. She is the most privileged and highest-placed girl in Denmark, he is her very well considered though nonetheless somewhat anonymous young friend, despite being her cousin.

For a long time he has felt a burning love for her, a love that he knows is hopeless and so has not expressed. But he finds his love so difficult to bear in her proximity that he has decided to leave and fight in the Franco-Prussian War. On the day when they are to part, and as he is bidding her farewell, she happens, quite by accident—teasing and mocking him in all innocence—to attribute to him in jest all the feelings that in reality he has. When, afterward, she learns that she has accidentally revealed his secret and ridiculed it—or turned it into a theatrical performance, a comedy— she is seized by feelings of shame and by a desire to atone. She sets up a complicated arrangement, which I need not go into, that brings her and Ib together in her aunt's living room, and there she offers him the relationship that she now feels she owes him, that is, a love relationship. And he answers, again for reasons that are not important here, that he cannot accept. He would rather die, he says. In other words, she meets with a refusal; she has worked herself up to an offer greater than any she has ever made before, but she is turned down and forced to walk away from him.

And as she walks, she has the following experiences— I take from the following paragraphs the passages that are most relevant for my purposes. She begins by being very angry at Ib because of his refusal.

Her indignation and anger were felt physically, as an unbearable pain in the abdomen. The center of her fair body, from which sweet content should have flowed to all her limbs, was clenched like a fist, and she bent double under the pangs like a dry leaf crumbling in the frost, and with all her strength had to hold back a long cry—*"Es shwindelt mir, mir brennt mein Eingeweide!* [The quotation is from *Wilhelm Meister.*] After a further hundred steps, Ib's face suddenly mounted in front of her as she had seen it when they had taken leave of each other. At that the suffering changed place and character. In a big leap it mounted to her breast, constricting her heart and sending out tentacles into her shoulders and arms, to her elbows and wrists and to her little hands. (P. 308)

Then follows a long passage about the experiences connected with the pain in her heart.

Once more the pain in her body mounted. For a few moments it squeezed her throat so that she did really believe she was going to die; then it went up still higher and settled behind her eyes. It was no longer her own grief only or Ib's grief; it was the sadness of life itself and of all living things. It pressed upon her eyelids; it filled her with tears like a vessel overflowing. If she did not weep, she must die. (P. 310)

What is occurring here is an upward flow of energy through her body; beginning in her lower body, near the sex organs, it rises up to the heart, and from the heart up around her throat, and finally it comes to rest in a spot familiar to all who have seen the red dot that Indian women wear above the root of their noses. One need have only the slightest acquaintance with theosophy or anthroposophy, yoga, Freemasonry, or Tantric art to know that the places in the body mentioned in the above passage correspond to what in the Indian tradition—in Danish there is no word for it—are called *chakras*, a term that literally means wheels and that refers to the organs of clairvoyance and for the distribution of inner currents of energy that form the basis of the esoteric lore of all religions. Just as earlier we were confronted with the halolike light around Erik Glipping's head, now we are faced with a similar phenomenon, of which there are countless examples in Karen Blixen's writings. One thing is to notice that they are there; another is to realize that they always appear and make themselves known to consciousness at the very moment when destruction is at hand. Here Adelaide becomes aware of these previously unknown organs in the instant they are being destroyed.

It is the case throughout Karen Blixen's writings that this organic foundation or—what shall I call it?—this intermediate layer in human beings between their consciousness and their physical body is always a factor but equally so a limit. It is the zone where the great catastrophes occur. But it is also a zone about which one is not given very much information in her writings; for that one would have to look in an entirely different direction. In Karen Blixen, it is the zone that manifests itself at the moment when disaster occurs. Countless people have devoted their lives to the study of these remarkable phenomena; one can say that the entire Eastern tradition is centered around them. On almost any statue of the Buddha one can see delineated the currents and centers of energy discussed here.

I became aware of these phenomena through Karen Blixen's writings, but at the same time I came to realize that concerning them the tales would take me to a certain limit and no further. Rather than tell the reader about them, she uses them to stage shocking and dreadful experiences. While I still knew Karen Blixen, I tried to inform myself about these experiences. On one occasion I took along a book; I felt that somehow she had authorized me to do so.

The book was *The Secret of the Golden Flower*, a translation of an ancient alchemical text by the sinologist Richard Wilhelm with an introduction and commentary by Carl Jung. In it there are some Taoist meditation images in which the chakra points are depicted. I showed it to Karen Blixen, and, quite untypically for her, she instantly shoved the book back at me and would have nothing to do with it. I did not understand her reaction, because at that time I believed that

Karen Blixen's life was somehow involved with esoteric matters that were completely new and unknown to me. On another occasion, perhaps around the same time, she said to
me: "Now the relationship between us is such that you can
ask me anything. No matter what you ask me, I will give
you an answer. And, for your part, you can tell to me whatever you want." And so I asked her a question about some
of the phenomena I had found in her books. She fell silent
for five minutes, and at last she said: "How is your son,
Morten?" And that was all we said about that. On this topic
she remained completely silent.

Once one is aware of these things and tries to follow
their trace in her writings, I believe (I am sufficiently familiar with her writings to think that I am not mistaken in
this, but I have not made a thorough, sentence-by-sentence
investigation) that there is no esoteric material in her writings from the 1920s, not in the marionette comedy nor in the
story "Carnival" which, according to Frans Lasson, she intended to have been included in *Seven Gothic Tales*. But it
is present some years later, when the Gothic tales are published. I cannot differentiate between literary chronology
and biographical chronology here, but nevertheless I feel
fairly certain that many of the experiences that would be
relevant in this context date from her early life. An amazing
qualitative leap takes place in the period between the late
twenties and 1934, when she finishes her first book. This
becomes evident if one places "Carnival" and the marionette
comedy *The Revenge of Truth* beside the Gothic tales—a
leap that seems to have taken place once she was able to use
some of her experiences in a story. Then it was as if she had
punctured one of the large complexes that can weigh on an
author until he or she finds a way to get access to it. In
Karen Blixen's case, a great artistic liberation occurred; but
the organizing process that allowed her to articulate her
inchoate experiences was itself a piece of organic reality—
that is, it intervened and altered the relationship among the
various layers of her consciousness.

These changes manifested themselves in the ample, brilliant, excruciatingly sharp stories she wrote in *Seven Gothic Tales*. Later they showed up in a more subdued way in *Winter's Tales*. Of the two collections, it is probably the latter that has the greater pedagogical force, because the characters in those tales are more ordinary and the events appear less autobiographical. They are free of the intensely personal atmosphere of *Seven Gothic Tales*. Then, turning to her *Last Tales*—not least of all the tale *Albondocani*—the pedagogical element is gone again, for these stories are concerned with rendering visible and personifying the forces that she had encountered in the dangerous intermediate zone we have been discussing.

What I have tried to sketch out here are the paths one is led to when one realizes that, while the expression "the pathways of destiny" can hover over Karen Blixen's tales like a solemn formula for obscure and inaccessible decision-making processes, her own investigation of these paths was full of common sense and reasonableness. It led down through deeper and deeper layers of consciousness to the very deep level where decisions are made, and then even deeper to a place that is no longer a level of decision but a world of power that in some unknown way is the base for, or is connected to, actions. In this perspective, people's decisions become moves in a game whose rules they do not know, and unexpectedly they are caught breaking rules that carry overwhelming events in their wake.

In modern academic language, one might say that I have tried to delineate a kind of "deep structure" in Karen Blixen's works. This was not my intention. It was not to make that kind of analysis that I sought out these pathways, but to gain information. And there are great quantities of precise information in her works, so long as one confines oneself to the intellectual area, the area of consciousness. But all information ceases at a tragic boundary where the intellectual area ends.

\* \* \*

In closing, I will first try to pull my reflections together so as to locate Karen Blixen in modern European literature, then finally summarize my own personal experience of her.

If one uses the most evident qualities of her writings to evaluate her, the ones usually taken into account when literary history is written, one finds it very difficult to place her. She is not like very many other writers, perhaps because of her unusual childhood milieu, her unusual education, and the books she was exposed to in her youth.

Characteristic of her stories is that they are set in specific periods and in meticulously described, albeit somewhat sugar-coated milieus; they are peopled by utterly distinct characters of easily identifiable social identity. Not for a moment does the reader sink into the stream of consciousness of these characters; they speak, and an omniscient narrator is fully informed about their thoughts. They function according to classical notions of the spirit and they utter truths in grand programmatic maxims, and for both of these characteristics her writings can seem antiquated. The expression that I believe Henning Kehler used about her, "*Family Journal* for highbrows," can seem not very far from the mark so long as one looks only at this surface. It is a closed universe, while modern literature may be said to define itself precisely by an absence of characters who possess an identity, a clearly delimited consciousness, and who express themselves in grammatically correct sentences. Where Karen Blixen depicts a closed, almost naturalistically simple world of surfaces, modernism depicts rationality in the process of dissolution.

But her world is not entirely closed. Downward it opens onto a dangerous deeper dimension. There one touches not only upon the organic conditions I mentioned earlier, but also upon violent psychic conflict. Much of the literature of her time, of course, was also concerned with these phenomena.

In James Joyce's *Ulysses*, for example, one can find, superficial differences notwithstanding (it is possible that

Joyce would have understood Karen Blixen, since he understood so well the symbolist plays of Ibsen's later years, where this same obscure and dangerous psychic/organic force erupts into the orderly bourgeois world), the same doubleness as in Karen Blixen's tales: on the one hand, a dry religious orthodoxy in parodical and caricatural form, and on the other, real and disturbing eruptions of those forces of which orthodox religion preserves the distant imprint. Similarly, around Lou Andreas Salomé, who was closely associated with both Nietzsche and Rilke, and subsequently also with Freud, can be found events of the most remarkable nature. One would have to call them religious events except that the people involved strenuously resisted any such interpretation. During her affair with Rilke, which one can follow in their letters, remarkable experiences happened to him, transformations in his soul and body that he indicates with precision in his anxious letters to her.

What is at work here is an eruption, at a critical point in the history of bourgeois Europe, of the forces stemming from the borderline between the psychic and the physical. They erupted at a time when the old traditions, the old morality, and the old religion had all lost their power over people's consciousness though not by any means over the social institutions, chiefly the family, in which these people had grown up. Lines of traditional piety had been engraved in their lives, though perhaps not by means of traditionally pious words. One need only recall Thomas Dinesen's book of memoirs, *Tanne*, to see that the same lines were drawn in Karen Blixen's life as, a little earlier, in Sophus Claussen's, Nietzsche's, and Rilke's. That is, they were all raised in an atmosphere of strict sexual propriety. It is true that they all liberated themselves at an early age, but did so as artists or dreamers. They became free in their intellects or imaginations, which are not subject to the restraints of other people, long before they made a real break with, or created a distance from, their childhood milieus.

Probably little of this is surprising or strange to contemporary people. It is a common experience today to grow up in a tradition, and inherited moral form, that is not prevalent in society generally and so is abandoned. But while many people make this break with tradition, few experience it so violently as Karen Blixen did. Like many other artists whose youth was spent prior to World War I, she devoted the rest of her life to preserving and exploiting her imaginative world in her art. Her life became one of respectable middle-class behavior on the one hand and, on the other, of instinct ruthlessly unleashed in the worlds of thought and imagination. For more than one of these artists and thinkers, imagination turned from the mild and helpful angel of twilight into a dangerous, alien power that reached into their psyche and ripped away that part of it that was its own source.

It is within this roughly sketched area, and from one standpoint, that Karen Blixen's books, by virtue of their precision and acuteness, are unlike anything else in modernism. Conversely, she shares with many artists of her time a focus on depth. It was a general preoccupation that manifested itself in works of vastly differing outer appearance.

The characteristic of religious experience in Karen Blixen's writings is that it is always seen and evaluated according to the criteria prevalent in the milieu where the action takes place and where social identity is a given. This naturally implies that when religious forces appear they are always destructive of the plans and expectations harbored by the social order. I think this is her authorship's deepest secret, its inner focus, for, as I mentioned earlier, knowledge of the world of religious experience that Karen Blixen, in her way, was familiar with has for many people been the goal of their life. But not for her. For her, such knowledge marks a borderline, a point where social identity is irredeemably destroyed. It is the place where the human being is ransacked. The story about Ib and Adelaide ends with Adelaide sitting in a cemetery where, for a while, she has been weeping. We are told that she is now resting in the only form of happiness possible for her, the open avowal to the world that she is a human being who has lost everything.

I once said, in a remark quoted by Ole Wivel, that there was a great sorrow in Karen Blixen, one that I, the moment I met her, felt dominated her being; and so when I later read these words about Adelaide, I took them not only as referring to the character in the story but also as a statement by the author about herself. Of course, to read in this way violates proper interpretative rules, but it fits nevertheless, for the simple reason that the central process of "Copenhagen Season" could not have been described by someone who had not experienced it.

In closing, I would like to take the previously quoted passage as one of the two points defining the picture that Karen Blixen has left me. I experienced her as a human being who had lost everything: she is the only person I ever met who gave me the impression of having built her life on the total and unblinkingly recognized loss of any kind of basis.

The second quotation that keeps her image clear for me is also from one of her stories; its reference is more personal. Though it contradicts the first, I have no problem with applying to Karen Blixen the definition Pellegrina Leoni gives of herself in "Echoes": "I am nothing but a messenger sent out on a long journey to tell people that there is hope in the world."

With these two quotations I can summarize and conclude this lecture on my relationship to Karen Blixen and on her place in modern European literature. Though these two quotations may appear mutually exclusive, I nevertheless believe that their contradiction can generate insight into Karen Blixen's life. I close my lecture by referring back to my opening remarks. The best way to understand Karen Blixen is not through people's memories of her, or through their books of memoirs in which she appears, but in her writings.

In her writings and in the curve of her oeuvre, her life is exposed in a way that it never was in personal relationships. Therefore, it seems to me that until an appropriate language and conceptual framework are created that would be capable of expressing the things that are in her books, it is not possible, nor is it appropriate, for those of us who knew her to tell anecdotes about our experiences with her, anecdotes in which we figure as eminently normal and sane and so appear as either too stupid to have understood what was going on or too lucky to have done ourselves much harm, or again as victims of intentions that at the time we were not capable of understanding but which in retrospect now seem to be worth the trouble of deciphering.

# CHAPTER 4

# The Guardian of the Threshold: On Karen Blixen's *Last Tales*

## 1. Identity

Some have seen Karen Blixen's genius as fully formed from the start. That could not have been possible, of course, yet if one considers her and her writings from the time of her homecoming in 1931 to her death in 1962, the view is not implausible. She had, throughout these slightly more than thirty years, already achieved her final form. This does not mean that her power of literary expression did not grow with surprising rapidity in the early part of this period, when she was working on launching her literary career. If one compares *The Revenge of Truth* and "Carnival" from the end of the twenties with *Seven Gothic Tales* from 1934, one can observe a leap in both wisdom and expressive power. Nor does it mean that she did not expand her literary landscape or alter her style and tone several times in these years. She continued to make changes and adjustments in these areas until the end; and even for her the problematic of having her fate tied to a public literary career brought along unforeseeable consequences. But whenever she moved into new areas or took up new people, it merely meant—even when she would have wished it otherwise—that the new places and the new people became drawn into the completed structures of her being and subjected to its rules.

One can see this process clearly if one tries to gather in one's mind all of the features of the last major character she created, Cardinal Salviati. He is the figure who runs through her final and uncompleted literary project, the novel *Albondocani*. The spokesman for the story's philosophy, he is himself the product of a story that has raised him above ordinary existence and turned him into a "guardian of the threshold." To review this remarkable man's qualities is to see not only that all of the lines in her writings meet in him, elevating him to the position of the family spirit presiding over all of her tales, but also that he bears a nearly identical likeness to the portrait Karen Blixen drew of herself in her letters to her brother Thomas, in 1926, the great year of her letter writing.

Thomas Dinesen married in the summer of 1926. On that occasion Karen Blixen wrote to him that she wished that his home might become the base from which "you set out for a real profession, what is known as a 'calling'; that here *you may see your personality expressed in action.*" These last, italicized words articulate with exemplary brevity the realism in Karen Blixen's view of life and the basic formula for her stories: that a person acquires an existence by expressing his being, by dealing with himself objectively, by externalizing his power so that it becomes visible in the mark it imprints on the world. It is a realism that, on closer inspection, cannot be said to be lacking in fantastical elements, internal contradictions, and indeed, a crushing contempt for what in Denmark is generally called realism. But that she could entertain such views, indeed raise them to mythical status, is because she retained a clear understanding that there is no road around other people's reality, and that it is by this common reality that everyone is ultimately judged.

The letter goes on to explain the implications of her wish:

Holger Drachman has a poem—for which he has been ridiculed, which goes something like this:

> *I hear in the night*
> *from the silent woods*
> *a cry like: Help me*
> *my God!*
> *I get up, listen,*
> *cannot sleep.*
> *Who am I?*
> *What do I*
> *look like?*

I think that he has expressed something real, true, here. In a way it is what one is always looking for in life. By trying to look inside oneself one can only catch a glimpse of it, or rather one sees the sketch, the model, of the house or the ship which is to be built; in one's work, one's activity, the impression one makes, or the relation one has with the rest of the world—people and ideas—one actually gets to know it, one somehow sees it face to face. Often one has to laugh at it, it is so far from what one thought it was, many times absolutely astonishing for oneself; it is like in my old parable about the man who "fell in a ditch, got up again, and there stood—a stork" ... reality transforms dreams according to its own calculations which are often far from "standard exchange rates", but it "sounds true, like a good Sovereign" [in English in the original], and so one accepts the transaction and acknowledges it, even is grateful for it.

When her friendly wish and good advice are explicated as they are here, they show themselves to contain the notion of self-development, individuation, which is nineteenth-century literature's most sacred concept, in fact the passionate idea that has brought forth what we call literature. "*Wie man wird, was man ist*," as Nietzsche said, how one becomes in the world of reality what one by natural inclination already is, like the oak from the acorn. But to call this a notion or an idea is to view it too abstractly, for though it is an experience that thought can dismember and analyze after the fact, in life it unfolds with the force of a persistent passion, driving its possessor to exploits and achievements, firing him with an all-consuming passion. In a subsequent letter from September, Karen Blixen discussed her nagging feeling of not having realized her potential, the same feeling that in all of her relationships became the goad that made her drive and hector herself, her cook, her natives, and even her own coffee plants toward perfection. It is always, she writes, "the same conviction that drives me on: the feeling of the great value of the divine—in talent, in individuality, in beauty— and the fear of seeing it destroyed or wasted."

This is the tireless desire to transgress humanity's known limits, to become an Overman, a myth, a turning point, a bearer of new tablets. Throughout nineteenth-century Europe this desire increased in strength while the restrictions on self-realization, both theological and moral, steadily lost their power over people's consciousness, although they long remained in effect in practical life. The limits originally placed on the free unfolding of the ego so as to secure eternal life for the virtuous and the elect eventually lost their theological credibility but continued to operate unchanged as safeguards of familial happiness. For a great many people this ethical system was inadequate. For them the demand for a larger meaning resonated in their lives as an uninterrupted, forward-driving, and insistent tone.

The drive to plunge from the realm of predetermined norms, enforced identity, and foreordained happiness into the realm of the natural human being, the realm in which talent and individuality strive for development and perfection, is what Karen Blixen in these letters calls Lucifer but in her tales calls God.

Now, while this passion for the ideal drove many other excellent souls—for example, Rimbaud, Nietzsche, Rilke— into attitudes of unceasing Excelsior high above ordinary existence, wreaking havoc first on their psyches and then on their minds and health, it moved Karen Blixen along a curve that by a strange parabola brought her back down to the surface of the earth. Fired by the negative force of rebellion, she nevertheless knew how to set limits, to exercise moderation. She never lost sight of the fact that other people, the world around her, reality, were all the solitary rebel's counterplayers and judges, and that together they would be the ones who, in the last analysis, would decide the worth of all of her efforts.

Thus it may seem that her rebellion canceled itself out, but in reality it did not. Against infinite desire she balanced a sober awareness of the sources of satisfaction, an awareness that the world is finite and that even dreams are subject to the law of gravity, and she somehow maintained both her desire and her sobriety so that neither cancelled out the other. This restless equilibrium, this wisdom that overtakes flight, this remoteness and presence of mind in the same glance—surely these are the qualities in Karen Blixen that have made her both unassimilable to literary movements and inscrutable to her friends and acquaintances.

The double movement away from and back to people is given characteristic expression in the very long letter, quoted earlier, of September 5 to Thomas Dinesen. There she writes about her "lack of relationships," about the odd fact that she had no intimate friends and that no one could draw near to her, a condition that no doubt was painful but was also one that in the final analysis she chose because she prized her freedom above all else:

> You know that I have said that I would like to be a Catholic priest, and I mean it—it is very nearly what I am—but he would have to be more than human if he occasionally did not give a deep sigh on seeing the lamps lit in people's homes and families gathered together. I will not say that I am, like Shelley: "One whom men love not and yet regret;" people do love me, I think, but they do not want or are not able to come very close to me,—no closer than Farah or

Pjuske,—and surely that is rather remote from real relationship, of the kind, for example, that you are presently
experiencing?

A few pages farther she discusses the possibility that matters
on the farm might possibly improve to the point where she
might come quite close to paradise, but then adds, "of course
not in the way that you are in paradise, for I am, as I said,
Lucifer's child."

If one places these different but contemporaneous state-
ments side by side, one can feel that things such as balance,
happiness, solitude, what people call "an occupation," are all
being maintained in a state of tense ambiguity: Lucifer's child
as a Catholic priest, total isolation and freedom imagined as
possible within the community of the Church, her remoteness from people, who can come no closer to her than Farah
or her dog Pjuske, versus her eagerness, her tenderness,
her self-sacrificing helpfulness when confronted by the di-
lemmas and needs of the people around her—just so long,
that is, as their need was not for her, for she belonged to
no one.

If we now turn back to Cardinal Salviati, who was not
introduced to the world in full format until the *Last Tales*
(1957), we see that the similarities between this solitary and
convivial man and Karen Blixen's more than thirty-year-old
self-portrait are so obvious as to be self-evident. In what
follows I will therefore place more emphasis on those passages where certain features have been made sharper and
consequences clearer. One difference, of course, clearly separates the early letter from the later story: Blixen had written most of her books in the meantime. What she had sketched
in a private letter in 1926 as her particular view of life and
tentative self-portrait she was now stating in the 1950s as
categorical human truths articulated by a public and well-
known author.

The cardinal introduces himself in "The Cardinal's First
Tale," which begins with the last moments of a lengthy
confession. A woman dressed in black has finished confessing

and is about to leave, but at the doorway she turns back and asks her confessor: "Who are you?" For the cardinal to answer, both must resume their former places; then the cardinal, in an almost unbroken monologue, gives an account of his life, his thoughts, and his place in the universe. His reflections amount to a discourse on the nature of the story. In what follows, I will interrupt the flow of his remarks and comment on them in a way so as to show their systematic progression.

The central message in the cardinal's discourse is simple, and he repeats it several times: mankind's deepest cry of anguish is: Who am I? All of the other questions that people in their uneasiness and anxiety pose themselves are simply screens against or variants of this single question. When it is answered, the person is saved. And the only thing with sufficient authority to answer the question is a story.

The power to transform people's nebulous dreams of themselves into viable external images, which in 1926 Karen Blixen attributed to "reality" or to the presence of other people, is here attributed to stories. Only a story can confer identity, only identity can grant salvation. Here it may be useful, before investigating the nature of the story in more detail, to try to determine the psychological place for that message.

One can find excellent reflections on this matter in Berger and Luckmann's book *The Social Creation of Reality (Den Samfundsskabte virkelighed)*. "We have stated," they say, just as if they had been presented with the cardinal's program, "that unsuccessful socialization poses the question: 'Who am I?' " This is not to say that they simply refer this pathetic question to the various medical institutions, for they are in no doubt as to the fallibility of every social universe and the limitations of its power. What they mean, and correctly so, is that the various social universes, despite their built-in inadequacies, are nevertheless primary in shaping an individual's identity. The first thing any social sphere does is to confer identity upon its members, even before the question of its function comes up. Consequently, identity does not originate in the moment when one begins to wonder who one is; instead, this is the point of rupture with one's unavoidable origin, the moment when one begins to protest against the identity one has been given without having asked for it.

Identity, say Berger and Luckmann, "is something arising from the dialectic between the individual and society." It is a product of socialization. First and foremost a human being becomes what other people say that it is. The authors repeatedly emphasize "that the individual does not simply take on other people's roles and attitudes, it also takes on their worlds. Indeed, identity can be defined objectively as placement in a specific world, while subjectively it can be acquired only by means of that world." What this means in practical terms is that one cannot be a departmental chief, a housewife, a grade-school pupil in general and in isolation, one can only be these things in a ministry, in a home where there are people to care for, in a school. To carry out a function is automatically to participate in its context.

Here there are two levels of definition that must be clearly distinguished. The first, that identity means placement within a context and that the context is acquired along with the place, is a general definition that is valid at every level of the process. The other definition of identity, as that of a role maintained within a certain, specific social space, is narrower, and in this discussion its only relevance is to refer to the point from which one breaks away. Berger and Luckmann do not make a particularly strong case for this latter definition. They state that in no instance is socialization 100 percent successful, nor is its success ever zero. Every individual experiences a gap between his objectively attributed identity and his subjectively experienced personal reality, and it is when this gap is experienced as intolerable that the dramatic question arises: Who am I?

We have now located the psychological place for the cardinal's thoughts about his identity and at the same time discovered that if identity can always be defined as a place within a context it is also clear that this context must contain some elements external to the social order. These latter are provided by the story, in the sense in which the cardinal understands it.

The cardinal shows this clearly by the series of simple stories that he cites as his examples. He mentions Romeo and Juliet, the "Hawk" from *The Decameron*, and Cupid and Psyche from Apuleius. During the discussion he indicates the points in the plot that give the stories their meaning. They are points where something unintended happens. For example, the moment when Gulnare exchanges her husband's old copper lamp for a new one, or when the young nobleman and hunter kills his hunting falcon to make a meal for his beloved, neither one knows what the lamp and the falcon are really worth. Or when Psyche accidentally spills a drop of hot oil on her sleeping lover's shoulder. In each case something comes into the story that changes its direction, but this element has no social reality even though one encounters it daily under the name of chance. A chance event is one that no one has instigated but that can seem to have a meaningful or intentional effect.

In these stories, which are all love stories, chance or a series of chance events has two kinds of effects. The first is to separate. Chance disrupts a situation of equilibrium in which the characters are contentedly enjoying some preliminary state of satisfaction. Then the lovers get separated from each other, and in order to move forward in their lives they must regain what they have lost. They must find a solution, show courage, withstand pain, display qualities that they may well have had earlier but have had no opportunity to display. Of course chance can often produce an effect that is purely and simply destructive. Or again it can offer some of the characters the opportunity to become something more than they were, to transform themselves by actively assuming their own latent qualities. Here chance works creatively, but only by virtue of the characters' potential qualities.

While chance can separate, it can also bring together, and only in the latter case do accidents assume the qualities of significance and hidden wisdom. In the three stories mentioned above, the lovers are reunited at the end, but not by an operation of their own wills. The reverse, in fact, is the case. External circumstances join their wills and wishes together, so to speak, and unexpectedly reunite the characters. The characters obtain their wishes, but in such an unpredictable way that it is as if higher powers have endorsed their desire. It has been validated in secret councils to which they have no access.

This is what the cardinal means by a simple and classical story. He means a chance event that separates the characters and moves them forward and then mysteriously unites them again, thereby supernaturally endorsing the potentialities of their human nature. An example of this type of story that shows its pattern more succinctly than any of the cardinal's stories is "The Lost" from *The Decameron.* A young man and a young woman flee from Rome together because their parents oppose their plan to marry. They are attacked by robbers and separated from each other, and then each undergoes life-threatening dangers and tests which, miraculously, both survive. Each in his or her respective place is advised by helpful strangers to seek shelter at a nearby castle where, against all likelihood, their paths cross again. When the lady of the castle hears the strange tale of their adventures she says:

> You know each other and love each other, and you are both friends of my husband, and so it is fitting for me to help you, all the more so since you intend to marry. It is apparently also the will of God, since on the one hand He has saved you from the gallows and, on the other, you from being stabbed to death and both of you from being eaten by wild animals.

Now, if we were to ask what answer the lovers in these tales have received to the question "Who am I?" a question that to be sure they have not asked, the reply is obvious. They can say at the conclusion of their story: I am this man's wife, or I am this woman's husband, thanks to a passion that heaven, God, fate, has ratified. So much, not more. It is the kind of confirmation that Karen Blixen in *Out of Africa* calls "a stork."

Comparable storks abound in older Danish literature. It was not difficult for H. C. Andersen, Carl Bernhard, and Mrs. Gyllenbourg to conjure them up. When the good people in their tales have suffered enough adversity and shown sufficient perseverance, the moral order of the universe intervenes to save them. For these writers, the inscrutable will of God was not, in fact, so inscrutable as to prevent them from calculating when and why it would go into effect. Whatever else chance might be, it is in any case a mental construct. To recognize chance as the activity of the secret Providence that presides over life is at the same time to interpret it and link it to human concerns. Chance is like a Rorschach blot, an empty potentiality in which each person finds varying dramatic pictures.

Once chance is seen as meaningful, it can be looked at in a number of ways. To a religious view, for example, arbitrarily selected events can be interpreted as messages from God that then must be translated into reality. Or to someone interested in power and unable to achieve it on his own, chance can offer a way of orchestrating a series of random events so that they appear to naive people as the working of God's will, for which they then are willing to offer their lives. This process has been portrayed in a number of classical Danish novels.

Historically speaking, a reversal in the interpretation of chance coincided with the advent of modernism in Scandinavian literature (ca. 1870). Previously, during the so-called Golden Age in Danish literature, chance was primarily seen as a metaphysical agency; but by the end of the nineteenth century it had come to be seen as a source of costly illusions. Karen Blixen was well aware of the history of the concept. Her cardinal, though he belongs to the first half of the nineteenth century, is not naive in this respect. In his story, as I indicated above, he regards chance not as offering a message but rather as an incitement to action.

Here and there in Karen Blixen's writings one can find

clear and unambiguous indications that the providential messages provided by chance originate in the person in question. Chance is a kind of grid that consciousness imposes on the surrounding world in order to understand itself. It is the detour consciousness uses to take possession of itself when its other concepts prove insufficient.

Thus Karen Blixen relates at the end of *Out of Africa* that one day when her private universe seemed to be undergoing a Götterdämmerung, she went out looking for a sign. As to the reasonableness of this she writes:

> Many people think it an unreasonable thing, to be looking for a sign. This is because of the fact that it takes a particular state of mind to be able to do so, and not many people have ever found themselves in such a state. If in this mood, you ask for a sign, the answer cannot fail you; it follows as the natural consequence of the demand. In that same way an inspired card-player collects thirteen chance cards on the table, and takes up what is called a hand of cards—a unity. Where others see no call at all, he sees a grand slam staring him in the face. Is there a grand slam in the cards? Yes, to the right player. (P. 368)

The same logic is invoked by the priest, Sune Pedersen, in the story "The Fish." In response to King Erik's question about an amazing coincidence he has just witnessed, Sune, with great presence of mind, replies:

> My Lord, one thing I know, and that is that all events get their meaning from the minds of the people to whom they occur, and that no external event is the same for any two men on earth. You are my king and my commander, but you have not made your confession to me and I do not know your thoughts. (P. 245)

To return to the cardinal in *Last Tales*: he uses nearly the same words to Lady Flora in the third tale:

But the human being, who in dead earnest challenges—not Heaven, for Heaven is not to be challenged—but her own nature, Heaven will not let her down. Through her own nature it will mightily answer her. She is right: she is a noblewoman, and it is she who will transform the things that touch or strike her—not the outside things that will transform her.

It becomes apparent, in other words, as one moves from the earlier, naive tales told by the cardinal about young lovers to the story he tells about himself, that his words have radically changed their meaning. The concept of identity has been raised several levels higher, for it now signifies the capacity to be met by, or to be united with, one of the immortal individualities living in the world of spirit. In a literal way, the cardinal's world has always been watched over by this kind of providential heaven. During the nine months he spent in the womb, his mother, Benedetta, was uniquely preoccupied by the wish that he "one day proclaim to the whole world the triumph of beauty and poetry and his own true identity: 'Now I know that I am Achilles!' " And even if she did not get her wish as such, it traced a path that the subsequent events in his life followed. A story like the cardinal's could no longer end with the simple triumph of love and the lovers lying sweetly side by side. For him it is a question of a stronger drive, the private passion to realize the self that no earthly force can withstand.

With this reversal, the nature of chance alters or disappears altogether. It becomes one with the house or the family into which a child is born and from which he derives his meaning and in which he finds meaning as such. Whereas the young lovers had to wait until puberty before they were drawn into a story, in the latter understanding of story, chance stands waiting at the cradle, ready to meet the newly born child with its imprinting, destructive, forward-driving power. The situation becomes exactly as the sociologists claim: a child develops into the person who others say that he is. But that process generates a text whose innermost meaning the adult desires to understand so as to be able to purge it of all the nonsense and small-mindedness that happened to get included. No longer can the act of creating and the process of being created be separated from each other.

The only unusual thing about the cardinal's story is that he has been given two theoretically irreconcilable identities by his parents. It happened in this way: He was born from the union between a young girl and a very old man, a rough old nobleman who married to ensure the continuity of his family name. In the first years of her marriage, after having given birth to an abnormal child, the wife, Benedetta, awakens to a sense of her own worth. This occurs through her discovery of the world of art and by virtue of a swooningly enthusiastic and spiritual love affair that she has with the castrato singer Marelli. When she becomes pregnant for the second time, both she and her husband make definite plans for the child's future. She decides to call the child Dionysus, after the god of ecstatic inspiration, so that he will become an artist. The father, on the other hand, wishes him to become a servant of the Church and wants to name him after the Church Father Athanasios, defender of orthodoxy. The conflict is resolved and both parents obtain their will when Benedetta gives birth to twins. The conflict reappears, however, when the castle is struck by fire and one of the twins—it is unclear which—is killed.

This child grows up like other children, incorporating his parents' rules and regulations as a kind of second nature long before he begins to think of himself as an individual. Self-awareness dawns in a human being when the desire awakens to dig down through the archeological layers of childhood and excavate oneself. One name for this process is remorse, another is psychoanalysis. Both proceed by way of a critical, readjusting, thematically questing movement of memory back through all of one's achieved attitudes and considered choices, some of which, perhaps, were not authentic, or fruitful, or compatible with one's innermost identity. The cardinal has not been able to undertake this process. He solemnly declares that "the gift of remorse has been withheld from the man whose circumstances we are now considering." Like Pilate, he is obliged to state that what he has written, he has written, and what he has done, he has done. This is logical, given the fact that the imprint he received in childhood came first from his parents but almost as directly from God. Thus he is of the people for whom, as he says, "the only way to salvation for people in a story is through the story."

Having thus been given two identities that normally ought to have excluded each other, he has become both an artist and a priest. The lady in black who hears the story of his childhood feels that she is able to understand that he "in one elevated and harmonious figure has been able to play the roles of two incompatible personalities on the stage of the world." But as she says this, he quickly interrupts: "Do not use that word, do not speak of incompatability. It can happen that you meet one of these two persons, speak with him, listen to him, confide in him and receive consolation from him—then once you have left him, not be able to decide with which of them you have met."

## 2. The Mask

This is not the first time in Karen Blixen's writings that two incompatible figures have merged inseparably with each other. It is not even the first time it has happened between a nobleman and cardinal. In "The Deluge at Norderney" we are told how Cardinal Hamilcar von Sehested was slain by his chamberlain Kasparson, who then assumed his master's role. The killing occurs in the first hour of the deluge that, in 1835, struck the island of Norderney. Kasparson, who among many other things is also an actor, takes on the cardinal's identity during the subsequent day's rescue work. With his head wrapped in bandages he is present everywhere, comforting the grieving, strengthening the courage of the rescue workers, and in general sustaining the hope of the populace. He performs all of these tasks with such convincing force that the deluge is later remembered by the people of the region as "the cardinal's deluge"; in the memory of the farmers and fisherman it seemed as if a great white light shone from the cardinal's person and went out over the dark waters.

When the rescue work must stop for the night, the false cardinal halts the lifeboat and gives his place to a peasant family, disembarking along with three spa guests into a flimsy hayloft. Once inside, seated in the hay across from the eccentric lady, Miss Malin Nat-og-Dag, he gives an account of his actions and the view of life on which they are based.

Miss Malin asks the yet-to-be-unmasked cardinal whether he believes in Original Sin, and this starts him talking. First he states his theological views and then goes on to reveal his real nature. He thinks it likely that there has been a Fall, but "I don't think that it is mankind that has fallen. I believe that it happened in the heavenly sphere. We are now serving a lower heavenly dynasty." He relates this fall in heaven to the French Revolution on earth. The former deity, in his view, was the Sun King, the present one is Louis Phillippe.

The distinction made here between the old and the new deity does not coincide with any recognized historical division—for example, between the Old and the New Testament or Islam and Christianity, even if a version of Christianity is somehow involved in the metaphor. On the one side of the division stands the "great daredevil," the old God of creation, the one "who created the stars, the oceans, the deserts, poets, Homer and giraffes," and "who does not care a fig for our ten commandments." He is worshiped when individuals show courage and genius, when they make a supreme effort to surpass themselves. Opposite this world of power and exuberance stands a human God faithful to the bourgeois moral order and endowed with all of the usual virtues of good people and with none of a grand seigneur's vices, a God who asks for no other recompense than his fair earnings. This God is honored by pious imitation, by static dependability, and in return he grants well-being to his worshipers.

It is likely that this grandly conceived vision of a heavenly Fall that fixed a boundary between divine dynasties does not spring so much from theological or historical speculation as from contrasting perspectives derived respectively from a Sunday in Rungsted and a safari in Africa. This surmise is supported by a passage in one of Karen Blixen's letters from Africa, where she encourages her brother Thomas to make fun of her with the following words:

> You have been a priceless idiot, a fool, a madwoman of a sort that you really do bear comparison to the Lucifer you speak about. With Lucifer's spirit still alive in the universe and represented on every side of you, you have let yourself become completely crippled by a kind, loving, wonderfully benign familial milieu consisting of, at most, the several hundred thousand people who live in humane, heartily tolerant Denmark.

Doubtless the chasm between these different modes of life lies behind her vision of the Fall; but Kasparson's theology has a biblical basis as well in the Book of Job. During his rescue work, "he spoke to them in a strong and clear voice and recited verses from the Book of Job." The great daredevil whom Kasparson serves is the same God who finally revealed himself to Job in order to assert the magnificence of his creation against the other's demand for justice.

Since the Book of Job is a persistent reference in the story, it might be appropriate here to point out that there is one school of thought that attributes to it a special position in the Bible. There are good grounds to believe that Karen Blixen was familiar with this view, though most likely not from the particular book I am going to mention. In Mme Blavatsky's famous *The Secret Doctrine*, the author writes à propos of the age of the signs of the zodiac that the Book of Job "is the oldest book in the Hebrew canon and definitely stems from a time before Moses." Disrupting the canon, however, is only one of the tactics Mme Blavatsky employs in her inveterate criticism of the biblical notion of God that runs through the four volumes of this work. On this point she invokes the Book of Job in a more outspoken passage:

> The Church claims that the devil is black; but in the Bible, in the Book of Job, he is called "God's son" and in Isaias the bright morning star, Lucifer. A consistent strategy of dogmatic cunning is implicit in the fact that the first arch-angel to emerge from the depths of chaos was called Lux (Lucifer), "Aurora's (or the manvantaric dawn's) shining son." The Church has transformed him into Lucifer or Satan because he is loftier and more ancient than Jehovah, and so he had to be sacrificed for the new dogma.

This passage is not entirely clear; nor is Satan in the Book of Job a figure of such attractiveness that the book can serve as justification for reinstating him in his old prerogatives. But otherwise her line of thought resembles Kasparson's, and if only it were the God of the Book of Job and not its Satan who was called Lucifer, the two would agree.

It is hardly an exaggeration to say that this point forms the true nerve center in Karen Blixen's work. These characters and this theology express a desire for an intenser life and a loftier courage, a thirst for depth and infinity that is unquestionably the passion in Blixen to which thousands of her readers respond. Equally fascinating is the characteristic direction she gives to this passionate desire, inflecting it into the forcefield of contingency where wildness, lawlessness, and fantastic luxury prevail.

This passionate conception, in other words, is what underlies Kasparson's exploits during the deluge. It is very different from—in fact, directly the opposite of—the views he must pretend to have, that is, the beliefs about God and the world firmly held by the farmers and fishermen whom he serves. They consider the real cardinal to be as close to God as it is humanly possible to come. And in the qualities for which he has become known—compassion, obedience, love of law and order—they perceive holiness, and from them they expect miracles.

Between his real beliefs and his façade, Kasparson must use his actor's art to build a bridge. Drawing on his passionate ambition for a great role, he takes on the identity of the famous cardinal, an identity in which passion and ambition are supposed to have been transmuted into love for one's fellow man. By mightily concentrating himself and his artistic resources he succeeds in portraying selflessness. For, as he says to Miss Malin, he is a bastard by birth and in his bastard blood seethes an arrogance that, while it makes him sensitive to the slightest insult, also fills him with a bitter love for the poor fisher folk and farmers who were his mother's people.

> I have never in this world loved anyone but them. Had they chosen to make me their lord, I would have served them my whole life long. Had they fallen down and worshipped me, I would have died for them. But they would not. They reserved their love for the cardinal. Not before tonight would they do as I wished. They have seen God in my face. After tonight they will relate that a white light shone above the boat when I was in it. So be it, Your Grace. (P. 76)

By this ruse, the talent and passion formerly demanded by the older God could be cunningly rechanneled into the piety and self-sacrifice required by the new one, and the humble adoration of the people could be enjoyed as submission to the power of one's own personality. "By your mask I shall know you," says Kasparson early in the evening. In the two sides of a public mask, two irreconcilable existences are fused into a seamless unity—though at the expense, it is well to remember, of the real cardinal's life.

Here the reader is being shown an operation by which one dimension of human existence is annulled and removed and its polar opposite chosen in its place. The slain cardinal represents the possibility of freedom from the passions and from the struggle for power and narcissistic rewards to which they are linked. One cannot say that Karen Blixen ever gives an adequate treatment of such liberation in her writings; on the other hand, she never treats it as a mere figment of the imagination. She is always careful in her stories to specify the moment when the world of one of her characters loses its higher dimension and the character his or her connection to the higher self. She qualifies these moments as ones of real loss; they are like death or an irrevocable departure. A remarkable honesty, disinterested and entire, is at work here, a refusal to minimize the loss of wholeness or the cost of the choices being made.

In *Winter's Tales*, the opening and closing tales about the author, Charlie Despard, are closely related to the one about Kasparson, variations on the same theme. The first, "The Young Man with the Carnation," treats the isolation of the artist, his withdrawal from human fellowship as he moves to a higher point of view, and the second, which I am going to discuss a little more closely, "A Consolatory Tale," concerns the corresponding movement back down—if not exactly to human fellowship, then at least to a necessary public. In the latter tale Charlie, suffering from a case of writer's block, meets an old acquaintance who tells him a story about masks. In it Charlie can find an inverted image of his own problem. He is in despair at being an artist and unable to find the consolation that he customarily derives from the Book of Job, namely that when God speaks in the whirlwind He is speaking in exclusive defense of the artist. As an artist Charlie feels he is like the Lord himself, but the thought does not help him, for at the same time he feels helpless in the hands of his public. They have the power to decide whether he exists or not. Here his friend Aeneas, who has wandered back and forth across the world, can offer him guidance.

The story is set in Persia and concerns the beggar Fath, a man who bears a remarkable resemblance to the country's crown prince, Nazrud Din. This prince is in the habit of walking around the town disguised as a beggar in order to

This gives him access to the people's faith and enrolls him in the only socially recognized institution capable of conferring spiritual identity. As a priest, his individual strength becomes part of and is extended by the Church's extensive power apparatus.

He is a literary artist with no written works. He uses living people in his compositions, turning their lives into stories. In these stories he intervenes to do the work of Chance, particularly that of dividing and driving forward, confident that the processes he has put in motion will be brought to their conclusions by higher powers.

He is the one in "The Cardinal's Third Tale" who assumes responsibility for the fact that Lady Flora, during her sojurn in Rome, "challenges heaven" by showing scorn for the holy rituals, for, as he says, "the person who in all seriousness challenges—not heaven, for it cannot be challenged—but her own nature, heaven will not abandon her. Through her own nature the All Powerful will answer her."

He is also the one, in the story placed between the cardinal's first and third stories, though not called the second, who advises the authorities to grant the condemned sculptor Allori's plea to postpone his execution for twelve hours. The condition he proposes is that they allow Angelo, Allori's favorite pupil, who is not accused of anything, to act as a hostage in his master's place in jail, and to let both the old and the young artist understand that one of them, in any event, will be executed at the designated time.

Angelo enters the cardinal's story, and before he leaves it again he succeeds in discovering who he is, for in the course of it he has met his higher self in the figure of the condemned apostle Judas. The proud and solitary Lady Flora, on the other hand, is enabled by the cardinal's art to reconcile herself not only to her sex and her physicality but also to the teaching of the Church. This happens when she contracts syphilis by kissing the toe of Peter's statue in St. Peter's

Cathedral, so that at one and the same time she can feel loved as a member of the fold as well as judged and condemned.

When the cardinal himself wants to describe his special art he compares himself to a bow and the people under his care to stringed instruments. Thus he can speak of himself as "this frail instrument which, itself mute, in the hand of its master can bring forth all the power and richness of tone which is hidden in stringed instruments, so that in his vocation he is both creator and instrument." As one who is both instrument in his relation to his master, but creator and awakener in his relation to people, he can emphasize the lofty, superhuman aspects of his unique situation. "Though he has no earthly wealth or power," he says,

> he has been given a tiny portion of omnipotence. As easily as a child at home ties up and releases his father's favorite dog, he knots the band of the Pleiades and looses Orion's belt. As casually as a child in its father's house issues orders to the servants, he unleashes thunderbolts so that they strike down and declare: Behold, here we are! (P. 21)

It is difficult to say what it might possibly mean to tie the band of the Pleiades or to loose Orion's belt, or how one unleashes lightning bolts; on the other hand, it is easy to say where these expressions come from. The mighty artist in question here belongs among those whom God thought Job unlikely to understand; nor could he. But what Job could not do, the cardinal can, and thereby—like the false cardinal in "The Deluge at Norderney" and like the poet Charlie Despard in *Winter's Tales*—he takes his place as one of the chosen and distinguished servants of the wild and powerful creator God before whom Job must bow.

But splitting apart solutions that no longer work and breaking up superficial harmonies are not all the cardinal does. He is also the one, at the beginning of the first tale, who gives the lady in black an identity through acts of integration and synthesis. He offers her an interpretation. In her confession she had mentioned a quantity of details "which were disjointed and internally contradictory." In his answers to her, he brings them all together into a whole. "Oh, not into an idyll," she says.

> I am well aware that I am in for a furioso—but into a harmony without a discordant note to it. You have shown me myself! I might tell you that you had created me, and that I had come to life under your hands, and surely it would have been both happiness and pain to have been thus created. But it is not so; my happiness and my pain are greater still, for you have made me see that I was already created—aye, created by the Lord God Himself and issued from His hands. From this hour, what on earth or in heaven can harm me? To the eyes of the world, it is true, I am standing at the edge of an abyss, or walking in a blizzard in wild mountains, but the abyss and the blizzard are the work of God and are infinitely and magnificently beautiful! (P. 4)

In this instance the cardinal is the initiate who knows that he can make use of a divine plan by an act of interpretation. He both creates and does not create the woman in black by assembling the elements of her story into a unity —as if he were interpreting a text—but to be able to do this he must know the outline of the whole in advance. By "whole" I mean a coherent order of existence that unfolds by necessity, so that simply to have a place in it is equivalent to being saved, even if that place will ultimately be swallowed up by a disaster. It is regrettable for the reader that the cardinal's answer to the woman in black has been given before the story begins, but it should be possible for us to deduce his view of the world without his direct guidance.

His view is Christian. Or if that is not exactly the right word, we can say that his view is closely tied to the Christian tradition. Christianity supplies the interpretative frame, but a frame from which the main character is absent and his place at its center is empty. However, the appropriate negative forces are present: the spiritual forces of revolt, of misunderstanding, of essential error, and these are as vividly apparent as the shining corona visible during a solar eclipse. The cardinal's story has points of resemblance to Peter's apostasy, Judas's betrayal, and Pilate's ambivalence, and by offering him an answer to the question: Who am I? these similarities are his salvation—or what he calls salvation. There is, however, something disturbing about the kind of salvation that always implies destruction: Lady Flora's syphilis, Angelo's dividedness, the disaster in store for the lady in black. Such salvation gives off a rancid odor. And yet, taken together, the fate of these characters has something edifying or sublime about it. It offers the reader the view of characters who are more than usually gifted, spiritual, courageous, or valiant in confronting pain. By their example an infinitely trivialized Christianity is lifted up into a remoteness where it becomes a reality that is an enigma for human passion. Solar eclipses are not without their usefulness.

In the same way as this ambiguous, veiled connection to sacred history produces a double effect on the reader of the tale—who is present both when the action takes place and when it is interpreted—there is also a quality in the cardinal that only becomes apparent when one sees him through the eyes of the other characters and from a place within their own stories. He is silent. He puts things in motion, but he gives no warning of their outcome. He is no one's caretaker, and the episode with the woman in black, where he offers explanation and guidance, is a unique event in his life. He is precisely as hard as external reality itself, which only in its guise of landscape gives any indication of where roads lead. What he does, once he has picked up the scent in the world around of the strong old passions, is to enter a person's life as an agent of divine chance and to put his or her soul in motion. Then he withdraws to the threshold of sacred history, which is where he lives. From this vantage point he waits with tense curiosity to see where the motion will lead.

That is why he calls himself the guardian of the threshold.

## 3. *Stories*

A story is a narrative about people who intervene in each others' existences. When several people's wishes or objectives meet in ways that are either mutually curtailing or enhancing, an action occurs that cannot be said to originate with any one of them. While each of the invented characters is accountable for his or her respective nature and deeds, it is up to the author to determine the outcome when all of their actions come together to form a plot. This outcome contains the meaning of the story (its moral, spirit, ideology).

Since it is the author's responsibility to determine the course of events, it is important that the authority for the story come from a higher source than private feelings or whims. Art is lawfulness within the imagination, and every good storyteller tries to subordinate plots to general law.

As long as the ancient symbolic universes still retained some authority, tales consisted for the most part in demonstrations of how God, Nemesis, and fate permeated earthly life and imposed order on the tangled affairs of human beings. After the decline of these symbolic universes, laws of more limited scope replaced them. The point of a story could now be to show how economic power or childhood trauma, overwhelming love or bourgeois rationality imposes its system of cause and effect on people. Storytellers could also try to have no meaning at all, and merely narrate lives that had unfolded in front of their eyes—on the principle that if the lives had actually occurred, they had to have been possible in the first place.

On first reading Karen Blixen, one can have the impression that in her world the metaphysical universe of Romanticism has been cast into a furnace and resurrected, so that it has been baked dry but come out with more burning colors.

That is not so. There is no hint of superstition in her. She is exact. Her stage is human consciousness, and her plots consists of the movements that occur there. The law governing these movements has already been mentioned—individuation, the law of the unfolding of the self—and her art consists in driving that process forward to the point where the most distant determinant of consciousness has been registered and linked to the visible, sensual world.

The sequence in her stories is as follows: the characters enter, impelled by their natural longings for satisfaction, then accidents and circumstances thwart them and require countermoves. The greater the scope of what her characters wish to encompass, the more they reveal themselves. When they have used up the last of their inner resources, the story is over. The end can often occur before they do anything decisive or before anything decisive happens to them. With many of her stories even the most careful reader can be in doubt as to how they end, because often they end not with an event but with a decision that only much later will turn into an action. Or sometimes there is no decision at all, only the clear awareness of the impossibility of making one; two mutually exclusive actions have both shown themselves to be equally necessary. In these cases the reader and the characters find themselves in roughly the same position. They have entered a game, as one also does in life, without knowing the rules. And the otherwise so-eloquent narrator will not reveal to the readers what she has kept secret from the characters.

The stories focus predominantly on identity. The opposite can seem to be the case, though, because her characters frequently lose the identity they had at the start of the tale without getting a new and better one in its place. Though it is understandable that they feel this as a loss, in reality it is not a loss. When their inmost souls have been forced into the open, the characters lose their inner coherence and are left standing, as if decapitated, before the wall of the future—like deep-sea fish that explode when they are brought to the surface. The process is one in which they gain in self-consciousness and genuine identity, but for them these gains can only be felt as enormous deprivations.

For the reader, on the other hand, who is attuned to the underlying point of these stories, they have their own kind of clarity and pedagogical force. It would be hard to find texts that delve more accurately into the most secret workings of the soul. Her stories tend to feature spiritual and idealistic people who, out of great innocence or unconsciousness, launch into well-meaning and altruistic projects without noticing that in so doing they are feeding the inner demons still in service to the ancient god of passions. Against their wills and unaware, her characters are dragged by the story's undercurrents into a reality that is deaf to their projects.

This plot structure is most apparent in Karen Blixen's "trivial" stories, the stories she wrote for American women's magazines to make money. They are more lurid than the ones she counted among her real works but they possess the advantages of clarity and simplicity. Among these apprentice works are stories like "Uncle Seneca," "The Proud Lady," and "Ghost Horses." Rather than these, however, I shall instead give brief interpretations of several more advanced texts, three "winter's tales": "A Country Tale," "Sorrow Acre," "The Fish," and the series of stories that I will call the cardinal's second tale.

Eitel, the young nobleman in "A Country Tale," from the time of his youth has had the goal of running his farm in such a good and equitable way that people will say that the peasants on his property are treated fairly. He wants to atone for the guilt left him by his father, who once forced a peasant to sit shackled to a wooden horse until he died. Eitel has succeeded so well that the king himself has held up his farm as a model; but still the idea of fairness so haunts him, waking and sleeping, that at last he has become a recluse whom both peasants and noblemen consider odd. With only one person does he have a happy physical relationship, and that is with the young wife on the neighboring farm with whom he is secretly in love. At the beginning of the story he tells her about his father and his inherited guilt.

"To cut oneself away from the past," he said very slowly, as if to himself, "to annihilate it, is the vilest of all breaches of the laws of the Cosmos. It is ingratitude, and running away from your debt. It is suicide: you are annihilating yourself in it. I have heard it said, or have read somewhere," he added and smiled a little, "that a thing be not true until it is twenty-five years old—almost my own age. I shall not, at the moment when I have become, truthfully, what I am, in cutting off my roots turn myself into a shadow, into nothingness." (P. 200)

But a scant twenty-four hours later, all of the biographical and philosophical premises for his declaration of faith have collapsed in a revelation of the past that renders his isolation complete and cuts him off from both the past and the future. At the close of the story he has become what he least wanted to be: a shadow, a ghost, a fool.

Similarly, in "Sorrow Acre," Adam destroys the order in his life to bring justice into the world. After a nine-year stay in England he arrives at his uncle's estate, his former childhood home. During the six months following his cousin's death, he has been the titular heir. But now his uncle, in order to assure his family line, has just married the young lady of the court who was to have been his son's bride.

The nebulousness of Adam's status and the lack of clarity in his feelings for the old house provide the motive for his return visit. At the moment of his arrival, however, events are happening that raise his personal problem up to the highest level, where matters of justice versus human life, and of past versus present, are at stake. A farmhand had been accused of arson. As neither his guilt nor his innocence could be proven, his fate was hanging in the balance when the boy's mother, Anne-Marie, approached the lord in tears to protest her son's innocence. The lord grants the mother's plea for her son's freedom on the condition that she single-handedly and in one day mow a field of rye that normally would require three men. It is this deadly test that is taking place on the day Adam arrives home, and it is in light of it that he comes to see his uncle with different eyes. While previously he had seen him as a fatherly friend and mentor, he now sees his uncle as a tyrant ruling with gruesome arbitrariness over people's lives.

A gradual transformation of Adam's views and concepts takes place throughout the day. At first he wants to turn his back forever on his uncle, his estate, and his country. He changes his mind, however, when he arrives at a higher viewpoint from which he sees his uncle as a little, lonely old man deserving of compassion. Then Adam is seized by the vague and turbulent notion that he can somehow hand over his, his uncle's, and Anne-Marie's fate to the prevailing justice in the world, to the lofty and mysterious powers of life, by a single, unifying act. In the same way as Anne-Marie is wagering her life for her son, Adam feels he can risk his life for his unborn son by abandoning himself to the passion that has developed in him during the day for his uncle's young wife. He acts on his impulse while his uncle strides up and down in the rye field as a witness to Anne-Marie's ordeal. Adam, up at the manor in the company of his aunt, feels that he is:

> . . . as much in the centre of things as if he had stood in the rye field itself, and as near to those human beings whose fate was now decided there. Anne-Marie and he were both in the hands of destiny, and destiny would, by different ways, bring each to the designated end.
>
> Later on he remembered what he had thought that evening. (P. 65)

This last sentence is the only one in the story that departs from its present time. The reader grasps the point that temporal distance has again caused Adam to change his mind and to remember his former elevated thoughts with bemusement. This is not surprising, for hindsight allows him to see how he has cut himself off from the possibility of ever taking over the farm where his son is growing up as the legitimate heir of his uncle, and how he has abandoned the woman he loves to her husband, an old man for whom she can feel nothing.

Karen Blixen once wrote me a letter about "Sorrow Acre." The occasion was that Johannes Rosendahl had sent her the manuscript of his book *Karen Blixen, Four Essays* to ask for her opinion of it and perhaps her endorsement. Now Blixen had a very high opinion of Rosendahl, but not of what he wrote about her, and she asked me—"You who more or less understand my thinking (God help us!)"—to discuss the manuscript with Rosendahl, under the pretext that she was ill. My advice to her, which apparently she followed, was that she should follow the same principle during her lifetime that she would necessarily have to follow after her death: never to correct or endorse anything written about her but simply to limit herself to an expression of gratitude for the attention, so long as it was friendly.

Her letter concerning Rosendahl is interesting in that it clearly shows that her stories constitute a distinct universe that cannot be incorporated or translated into another set of terms—for example, theological ones. It is also interesting in its suggestion that her stories are so calculatedly balanced, with such dangerous and difficult constructions, that not even if she were to point out a particular thread running through "Sorrow Acre" could it be allowed to be looked at in isolation.

In her letter she mentions two reasons why she has difficulty understanding Rosendahl's manuscript. The first, that he takes her too seriously, or seriously in an incomprehensible way, comes up in her discussion of the second:

> The second obstacle is that Johannes Rosendahl makes use of a terminology I am unfamiliar with. For us to understand each other, we would have to begin asking each other "What do you mean by this word? This concept?"—and attempt to arrive at a common definition. For example, "atonement"

and "salvation", which run through the entire book, or "punishment—justice". Even to discuss these concepts with Johannes Rosendahl would be disagreeable to me because he takes them so dreadfully seriously. I might end up by feeling, when I let one of my characters die, that I was accountable for committing murder or passing a death sentence.

There is a guttersnipe manner of making fun of things, and it is not pretty. But I have learned that there is a corresponding theological manner that gives the appearance of taking things seriously, but that in reality distorts them just as much, and when one encounters it one feels even more helpless than one does with the guttersnipe, whom after all one can give a swat on the side of the head.

Can you give me an example? Yes, see page 1: "The nobleman is, however, merciful and allows the mother to assume the son's place and atone for the offence." As I see it, this is a distortion.

On page 7, J. R. takes up Adam's conversion in "Sorrow Acre" by writing: "Salvation in Karen Blixen is immanent, in that it is granted when the gates of understanding are opened for Adam. He is obliged to hand himself over to 'the mightier powers of the world. Now what must come must come.' The exemplar and the disciple must pass through the same narrow gate, they are each others' equals, and an apotheosis awaits them both. That is their triumph. 'He himself would come to know ache, tears and remorse, and, even through these, the fullness of life.'" Yes, all of this is correctly quoted, and perhaps may even be said to be correctly understood, but it is such a difficult and dangerous thing to deal with "stories", and so unpleasant for the author, that she would actually much rather listen to the guttersnipe.

But to return to my solemn critic: "What role does Christ play in the story of Adam's conversion in Sorrow Acre?" And the author has to answer: "I hadn't thought that Christ plays any role, and was of the opinion that one could not decently allow him to." For in the final analysis Adam's conversion comes down to this, that rather than leave for America he decides to stay where he is and put a couple of horns on the old lord's head. In this way can his "abhorrence of the tyrant die out of him, and his pity for all creation extend even to the sombre figure before him." The old lord understands him to the extent that when he hears Adam predict that Anne-Marie's death and its consequences will be upon his head, he takes off his hat and runs his hand over his powdered skull and asks: "Upon my head? In what shape will it come upon my head, my nephew?"

Now I would just as little like to be held to this interpretation as to Rosendahl's. I might perhaps say that this interpretation is in the story—but the one must not turn the other into pure blasphemy. (March 21, 1955)

Running between the theme of destiny that Rosendahl emphasizes and the more piquant aspect of the plot that Karen Blixen points to in her letter runs a third line, which is perhaps the tale's real center. It is only very faintly indicated. At a certain point Adam informs his uncle that his peasants are people "who are simpler than you, and closer to nature, they do not examine or analyze their thoughts and feelings." Earlier in the story the narrator used similar words to characterize the young wife in the house: "She had no experience in analyzing her feelings; there had not been time for that at Court." When Adam makes love to her, thereby involving himself, Anne-Marie, and his uncle in the lofty and mysterious powers of life, he is starting to use her as an instrument, a fourth player in a metaphysical game of which she knows nothing, since she does not even know what is taking place in the rye field. Once she is involved, the pattern of the story is completed and at the same time changed. Adam no longer stands as Anne-Marie's equal in relation to the old lord, but rather as his uncle's equal in their mutual misuse of power over the two women.

More is at stake here than delicacy on a young woman's behalf. In Blixen's stories, sexual relations are the point where existence is infused with powers whose meaning transcends all idealistic notions, because sex gives consciousness its organic basis, which in turn determines its possibilities for experience.

Thus Adam listens utterly unmoved to his uncle's account of his strange agreement with Anne-Marie when he meets him that morning in the garden. He even sees the woman in the distance in the field of grain, but walks on up to the house. However, when he returns to the field later in the afternoon, after having spent the day in his aunt's company, he is in a different frame of mind than in the morning—in fact, different than ever, for now he is gripped by "a deeper, more heart-felt compassion with all living things than he had ever felt before." But at the same time he is troubled by a mysterious uneasiness that he associates with the drama in the field, a feeling of approaching unhappiness and woe threatening not only his uncle "but the house, the family and himself."

Now, Adam is no novice in erotic matters, but perhaps for that very reason he is not prepared to understand that love does not always manifest itself in the same way. Encounters can occur in the area of sexuality where the stakes are higher than usual, where the attraction between two people is directed by deeper forces of consciousness than those that can be temporarily assuaged by an embrace. In the course of the day spent in his young aunt's company, Adam feels his consciousness gathering itself in the region of his heart, producing a previously unknown radiation there. But by evening his intellectual awareness has reasserted its control and driven this energy back into his brain and his sex organs, two centers that for a brief moment had been about to merge. Trusting to his sense of justice, which is the intellectual's conception of love, he charms his aunt and cuckolds his uncle for the sake of reestablishing equality, and thereby achieves, as I mentioned before, no other equality than one between himself and his uncle, which is not what he had intended at all and which is the only thing, in his subsequent exile, that he has to look back on.

This erotic theme, so central in Karen Blixen's writings,

is elaborated even more clearly in the tale called "The Fish."
In fact, of all of Blixen's stories, this is the one that reveals
most paradigmatically her imaginative universe and her notion of the stages of psychic development. Contributing to
the exemplary quality of the story is the fact that its historical milieu, Danish early Middle Ages, lies far from her
preferred time period, 1770 to 1900, and consequently for
her it is also much vaguer in contour. Drawing primarily on
folk songs, she creates a form shaped almost entirely from
within that unfolds with fairy tale or archetypal simplicity.

The movement of the plot is linked to one symbol, a
ring, which is moved about and transformed. The story begins with the king, Erik Glipping, lying awake one summer
night, overwhelmed by feelings of loneliness and isolation.
He feels he has no equal on earth, and the joys of love that
he used to have with the ladies of the court no longer tempt
him. The wine no longer exists that might make him glad.
His thoughts move around, searching, and then upward in
their quest for a peer. They do not rest until they come to
God, an even greater and necessarily lonelier king. Then his
thoughts take a gentler turn toward the Blessed Virgin Mary,
whom they humbly approach: "No, no, Lord, I should have
but worn her glove upon my helmet."

In a violent act of decision that causes something within
him to break with tremendous reverberations, he tears himself away from the world of kingly duty that has become
empty for him:

> "O Lord, it is time," the King thought, "that I should turn
> away from them, that I should throw off everybody that
> stands in the way of the happiness of my soul. Of that only
> will I think. I will save my soul; I will feel it rejoice once
> more."
>
> At that moment it was to him as if a bell were ringing
> in the summer night, which no one but he could hear. Its
> waves of sound enclosed him, as the sea a drowning man.
> The King rose on his knees in his bed and lifted up his
> face. He knew and understood everything. He saw that his

loneliness was his strength, for he himself was all the earth.
(P. 229)

At that instant the king gives up his power and lets go of his inner world; henceforth it comes to meet him as external event. He has no notion of the necessity he has put in motion.

When he wakes the next morning he finds himself thinking about his father's old Wendish slave, Granze, a man skilled in witchcraft. In line with the previous night's decision that made him a free man, no longer bound by propriety, he dismisses the nobles waiting to see him and sends word to the queen, who had requested his presence, that she can expect him the following day. At the moment, he wants to find Granze. But before he departs he is visited by the playmate of his youth, the young priest Sune Pederson of the Hvide family, who has just arrived home from his studies in Paris. The king invites him to come along, and together the two mighty nobles ride out from Søborg castle through the woods and down to the shore at Gilleleje, where Granze lives.

Sune, who is an alert young man, quickly senses the bizarre and dangerous qualities of the king's behavior, and he cautiously tries to counsel him as they ride along. His efforts fail, however, for his heart is not really in it; he is haunted by memories of Paris, which inspire him to think about paradise. What he is really thinking about remains unclear, but there are hints in his talk of a chaste, eager, adoring love for a noble lady who has captured his thoughts. Sune's tender secret becomes the pivot upon which the subsequent action turns.

When the two riders halt on the dunes, Granze sees them from the seashore and goes to meet them. But he directs his greeting not to the king, as rank would require, but to Sune:

"Is it you who have come here, Sune, kinsman of Absalon?" he said. "I thought you were dead." Smiling on his high horse, Sune shows he is quite alive. "You came near to it, though, seven full moons ago," he said . . . "A woman cooked a nice dish for you," he tittered, "and put ratsbane in it. Did she take you for a rat, little Sune? If the rats would go into the holes that God made for them, people would not poison them." (P. 239)

Now the smile has disappeared from Sune's face; he is pale as he sits on his horse without a word.

What has happened during this welcome becomes clear only later in the story, when Granze says to King Erik: "Now I shall tell you why I was afraid to speak to you when I first saw you. As you came over the downs you had a shining ring around your head, such as your holy pictures have. Where did you get that?"

One notes the tense of the verb *had*. The ring that the king had around his head a short time ago is gone; it disappeared during Granze's conversation with Sune. In the instant when Granze turned Sune's heart inside out and scornfully tossed his precious dream down on the sand, the king's mood changed, too. For he, too, during the night, had adoringly approached a noble lady, the heavenly Virgin. That was when he acquired the shining ring which now has been extinguished by the mockery flung at Sune, "the little man of God," with his sweet and delicate desires. In this way Granze has struck his real target, though he directed his blow at Sune as the one less dangerous to insult.

The thing itself, the shining ring, is not so unusual as some might think. Similar wild haloes have, for longer or shorter periods of time, been worn—or mistakenly not worn—by all of the great artists who achieved their greatness through sublimation: Baggesen and Grundtvig, Ibsen and Claussen. On some of Willumsen's self-portraits one can even see it with the naked eye. As his friend Sophus Claussen said: "Nothing real can be erased by force; it will come back again, perhaps in an unexpected form." This is what is happening here, and happening more than once. When desire is blocked by a wish for something more than desire, something higher, nobler, the highest self, then the subtle components of desire rise upward to show themselves as a halo around the head.

No sooner has the ring disappeared than it reappears —now coming from the sea, in the stomach of the large fish Granze caught that morning. As Granze cuts it open and sticks his arm into its stomach, Sune thinks of the recent moment when it was he who had Granze's hand in his intestines, but the instant he sees the ring he again becomes the moral, wide-awake, and intelligent Sune. He compares the king to King Polycrates, who threw his signet ring into the sea to diminish his own luck but had it brought back to him the next day in a fish—and shortly afterward was killed, because others found his luck to be too dangerous in the world of human order. " 'But I,' said the king after a moment, 'have not tried to get rid of my luck by throwing my treasures into the sea.' " He does not remember the break he made with the world last night as well as Sune does his; it is unclear for him. However, the king is right in the sense that it is not his ring that appears out of the sea; the ring belongs to Fru Ingeborg, Sune's cousin, Stig Andersen's wife. Sune recognizes it with wonderment. He saw it a week ago on her hand when he was sailing with her in the waters around the island of Hielm. In his mind's eye, the king sees the boat sailing into the light breeze, "in the bow a fair lady, in silk and gold, her white fingers playing in the ripples, and underneath them the big fish swimming in the dark-blue shadow of the keel."

Up from the sea's great unconscious rises a ring and the name of one woman to which the king can attach the vague desire that until now has been submerged but is now liberated, as he is liberated. From being a possibility for inner growth, his soul now comes to meet him in the figure of a real woman who can be forced and conquered. The fish, that is, *piscis* and a symbol of Christ, now takes on its second significance as a sexual symbol, and the king slips unresistingly into erotic fantasies about Lady Ingeborg.

At that moment the two friends also let go of him, Sune playfully and Granze with almost ritual seriousness: "Now the fish has swum, and has been caught, now it is fried and ready to serve. It remains but for you to eat it; your meal is here for you." The way is now clear for the king's sexual possession of Lady Ingeborg and beyond that to his death in the barn of Finnerup.

As the final story in this series we can place the one about Angelo, the cardinal's second tale, which, like the others in which Albondocani figures, is told in an abstract, elevated style appropriate only for matters of ultimate importance, so that the events of the tale take on a paradigmatic quality.

Angelo is a young artist and the favorite student of the famous old master Leonidas. For him, Leonidas is the incarnation of "the highest thing in the world," great art, and he sees him constantly "surrounded by an aura of light from the highest sphere, from the infinite space of spirit and great art." As the epitome of everything Angelo is striving for, Leonidas represents the way and the key to Angelo's own universe, and he has no other name for his jealous admiration and total dependency than love. But if it is love, and perhaps it is, it is not of the subservient kind. It does not prevent Angelo from falling in love with his master's young wife, Lucrezia; rather, it provokes and focuses his passion. Only by uniting his art and his love in this way can Angelo feel himself to be whole. Lucrezia responds to his insistent desire, and their story, in which betrayal is heaped upon betrayal, begins with the two young lovers secretly agreeing on a place where they can meet and make love.

In this shattering prelude the tale's recurrent theme is introduced, from which it has also taken its title: "The Cloak." This garment symbolizes (as, by the way, does the shift in "Alkmene") the vegetative zone, the level in the human organism known in esoteric terms as the ether body, that is, the area where the sexual energy responsible for individuation and identity is located. This zone is activated in Angelo by his adamant desire to become master of himself and the spiritual light he intuitively perceives around his master. So rapt is he by the dream of gaining access to his inner self that even when Leonidas is arrested, accused of treason, and condemned to death, he barely registers the information. He is preoccupied solely by his immediate future. He goes about in a state of solitary intoxication "as if he had not heard or had not understood the terrible news." Before Leonidas's arrest, however, Angelo did notice that his master was making changes in his routine. Leonidas, for his part, suspecting that he was about to be accused, finds a pretext to have Lucrezia move to a friend's vineyard in the country. This causes the two lovers to look at each other "in triumphant certainty that now, and from now on, all powers of life were uniting to serve them, and that their passion was the loadstone which according to its will attracted and ranged everything around them."

That higher powers are operating around them may be true enough, not only because the cardinal is about to enter their story but also because Leonidas is informed of their feelings and intentions. He is so partly because the two had made their plans in Lucrezia's living room beside his atelier "while the door was open" and partly because he is fully able to hear and repeat aloud the things that Angelo speaks silently to himself; so close are the two men to each other that the otherwise normal boundaries between them have broken down, which also explains why the one is mistaken for the other entering or exiting the jail wearing the same cloak.

The deep affinity between them showed itself earlier in their profound mutual attachment to Lucrezia's beauty; it brought them together in the sense that, while painting Lucrezia, Leonidas invited Angelo to paint a competing picture. The moments in which she was both everything and nothing for the two men gave Lucrezia a painful insight. She glimpsed "at the same time with a kind of dismay and giddiness—the hardness and coldness which may be found in the hearts of men and artists, even with regard to the ones whom these hearts do embrace with deepest tenderness." The artistic drive thus activated in the two men is what drives the plot from that point forward.

After Leonidas has been condemned to death and his execution scheduled for the following Sunday morning, he asks the authorities for twelve hours of freedom in which to bid farewell to his wife. His request is denied, but Cardinal Salviati arranges that he be temporarily freed in exchange for a hostage, and Leonidas chooses Angelo. These arrangements are accordingly made.

Angelo comes to the prison in his new cloak, now entirely focused on carrying out his appointed mission of honor. After the men have embraced and Leonidas has thanked Angelo for the hours he has given him, Leonidas begins to pronounce with insistent, dignified intensity his final, deeply felt words to his beloved disciple. He speaks first about faithfulness, "the supreme divine factor by which the universe is governed." Then he counsels Angelo to remain faithful in his heart to the divine law of proportion, the golden section. But only when he solemnly and passionately declares his intention of going to Lucrezia's house, repeating point for point the plan of the two faithless lovers, does Angelo recall that this is the night Lucrezia is expecting him.

As Leonidas leaves the prison wearing Angelo's cloak, the memory of his words rouses forces in Angelo that violently shatter the cheap, illusory harmony he has been briefly enjoying.

No longer love for the unobtainable Lucrezia but an indomitable physical jealousy seizes him, almost choking him, and giving him bloody, murderous nightmare visions. "The son's raging hatred of the father" makes him gnash his teeth in the dark. Then suddenly his violence and wrath give way, not to admiration for his spiritual ideal but to shame about the way he has betrayed him. All night the two contrary powers tear at him, sharpening themselves one against the other, distorted desire against remorseful self-consciousness. Thus when Leonidas returns in the morning, with a single stroke he can seal the night's work and cut the golden section into Angelo's heart. As he, the powerful magnet in Angelo's universe, is draping the cloak over the young man's shoulders, he places his hand at the nape of Angelo's neck and pulls his head a little forward, thereby raising the kundalini power in Angelo in the same way as it has been raised in himself. Then he kisses him and they part with no further words.

In "Night Walk" we are told about Angelo's life in the time immediately after Leonidas's death. The person who formerly gave meaning to his life is gone. He finds himself in a world lacking in all direction. Worse yet, he can no longer sleep.

In the beginning he experiences his insomnia as his own choice, a condition confirming him as an exceptional person. But after it has lasted for a while it begins to have a destructive effect on him. "But, just as unexpectedly, his body rose in rebellion against his mind and will. So that he became, in ways more painful than he would have thought possible, divided and troubled. Before, all the parts of his nature had lived in happy harmony with each other, when one part called, another responded"—but now his body revolts like a bucking horse trying to throw off its rider. At last he is forced to bow to the needs of his body and to pray to the powers to let him become like other people and be able to sleep again.

He asks people for advice on overcoming insomnia and is given many kinds of mental exercise before he finds one that is effective. But by this time he is so fatigued that he prefers to exercise on foot rather than in bed. He circles through the town, turning into progressively narrower streets until he arrives, half awake and half asleep, in a narrow alley in front of a closed door—a sort of backwater of reality that is real enough but that in a way is outside of waking, ordinary, physical life. Trying the door and finding it open, he enters. Inside he finds a red-haired man seated at a small table counting silver coins. The man is ugly but his door is open.

"After a while Angelo said: 'I cannot sleep.'

The red-haired man looked up. 'I never sleep,' he said haughtily."

After a short while he explains his painful privilege. "Only dolts and drudges sleep," he says. Then, full of contempt, he proceeds to relate how the other disciples slept while the master was sweating drops of blood in deadly terror only a few feet away from them. " 'But no one,' he concluded slowly, in indescribable pride, 'no one in the world could ever seriously believe that I myself did sleep—on that Thursday night in the garden.' "

Ambition and adoration, two seemingly incompatible attitudes, come together here in a way that reveals that to be the chosen disciple or the rejected traitor are not two mutually exclusive or self-cancelling conditions; indeed, they have come together in one figure, in one violently intense face—into which Angelo is compelled to stare in recognition of the very self that, by force of ruthless and inveterate effort, he has become.

The third segment of Angelo's story, "Of Secret Thoughts and of Heaven," takes place seven years later and is a kind of stocktaking: what has been the result of those fumbling, exciting, and raging years of his youth? Angelo is now a rich and famous sculptor sought after by princes and cardinals. He is married to Lucrezia, and they are expecting their fourth child. He is more handsome than before, his great beauty now "blossoming almost like a woman's."

One evening, while sitting on the terrace in front of his house modeling some clay figures for his children, he receives a visit from Pino Pizutti, an acquaintance from earlier, leaner days who is a puppeteer and philosopher with whom he enjoys discussing life's great questions. Twice during the conversation Angelo is surprised by Pino's words, first when he says: " 'I have loved since last we met.' 'Loved?' Angelo repeated, slowly and with astonishment, as if he were repeating a word in a foreign tongue." And, second, when Pino asks him if he is able to sleep. " 'Sleep?' Angelo repeated, again as if sounding out a word from another language. 'Aye, do you remember when I could not sleep? Yes, thanks, now I can sleep.' " The bygone years have almost vanished from his memory, he has found his balance, and there is nothing in his present, easy life for which the word *love* would be appropriate.

And when at last, after assessing his own prospects for getting to heaven, Pino turns to Angelo: " 'And you yourself now,' he said after a minute. 'Are you going to Paradise? And shall we meet and talk together there, as we do here now?' " Angelo sits for a long time in silence, trying to see if there is a pattern in his life, but he finds none. " 'A man is more than one man,' he said slowly. 'And the life of a man is more than one life.' " He sees the years of his life as distinct blocks: the utterly self-absorbed young artist, the sleepless and despairing night-walker—and now the mature and famous sculptor, the eminent teacher, the good husband and father. These three men are like Jesus and the two robbers who were crucified together. An old topic of conversation between him and Pino used to be which of the two robbers each of them might be. But now, as I said, Angelo's life has fallen into three independent existences. The young Angelo, he says, could not have gone to heaven, for he was too light, he could not have risen so high. Nor could the present mature Angelo go to heaven either, for the simple reason that he no longer wishes to. He has everything he wants on earth. " 'But,' he finished very slowly, 'the young man whom you met at the inn of Mariana-the-Rat—the good home of thieves and smugglers down by the harbor—the young man with whom you talked there at night, Pino—he will go to heaven.' "

Implicit in the statement that places the insomniac and unhappy Angelo between the two others is a belated recognition that when he betrayed Leonidas he betrayed himself, and that what he lost during that period of erotic confusion and inner strife was his innermost self—the self that might have made his life whole.

Looking back over the four stories I have just discussed, we find one significant and recurrent characteristic. All of the stories are about men trying, each on his own level and with great effort and sacrifice, to become themselves. What that self is, is unclear, but it is something conquerable that is both dangerous and alluring. And in each case a woman is either pushed out of the man's life or drawn into it as something they know all about and can work with, depending on what, from a higher standpoint, is appropriate. Sometimes clearly, sometimes subtly, but unfailingly, the moment is noted when the woman is painfully deprived of her existence. It is clearest in Angelo's story, when Lucrezia, with a kind of horror, feels herself to be both adored and annihilated by the same intense artistic glance. This doubleness is also present in Leonidas's farewell speech, when he solemnly describes the final night he is about to spend with his wife: " 'I tell you, Angelo, that in order that man—His chief work, into the nostrils of whom He had breathed the breath of life—might embrace and become one with the earth, the sea, the air and the fire, God gave him woman.' " The doubleness is again present in Angelo's thoughts during his night in prison, when he painfully realizes the cost of the object for which he has sacrificed his fidelity to Leonidas: " 'And unfaithful,' he thought after a time, 'for the sake of a woman. What is a woman? She does not exist until we create her, and she has no life except through us. She is nothing but body, but she is not body, even, if we do not look at her.' "

There is much more in these examples than the mere recognition of the extent to which women and womanliness are denigrated and misused. These stories are about all that can become visible for men when women become invisible, about all of the unsuspected forms that love can assume in men who walk heedlessly past it. Of course the stories give only the negative consequences of this misrecognition: the destruction, the illusions, the mistakes. The space of these tales is one filled with the shadows of a reality of which one glimpses, at most, only its heel at the moment of flight.

Given this point of view, one can take comfort in the fact that the stories remain hypotheses, by which I mean that they presuppose that at their conclusion the materials from which their characters are composed will have been exhausted. Putting it differently, one might say that their logic is based on a determinate amount of vital energy and capability to change, which are their postulates. Herein lies their limits and their usefulness, for otherwise they would be nothing but condemnations, life sentences. They are much more than that, and their stringency, like a canal lock, allows them to become channels of transit and progress. That is their usefulness and their pedagogical significance; they are solutions to riddles one could never have posed, even while being involved in the riddles. And, finally, they are heart-breakingly colored by the kind of happiness that can radiate from a person who herself never was happy.

## 4. Pellegrina

The most difficult fairy tale in all of Karen Blixen's writings is the one about Pellegrina Leoni, which she tells in two stories, "The Dreamers" and "Echoes." There can be little doubt that the sophisticated and at one time famous novel *Trilby* (1894), by George Du Maurier, served as a kind of model for the story. The novel is about a Parisian model, the *amie* of several students, who, under the magnetic (mesmeric) influence of the demonic Hungarian musician Svengali, becomes a famous opera singer, but loses her voice when he dies. But as was so often the case with Karen Blixen, rather than limiting her imagination, the model worked as a stimulus, so there is little point in comparing the two works. As Charlie Despard says after he has heard Aeneas's tale about Fath and Nazrud Din: "Yes, a good tale. . . . No, not a very good tale, really, you know. But it has moments in it that might be worked up, and from which one might construct a fine tale."

With the figure of Pellegrina, Blixen apparently intended to extend a seldom-discussed line running through nineteenth-century Danish literature. If one looks from Baggesen to Grundtvig and from Grundtvig to Claussen, one can follow the progress, as if in a relay, of a strangely ambiguous, ominous figure of a woman who is both destructive and life-giving. She moves forward through their collective imaginative space and assumes an increasingly lifelike appearance as she advances. Now, it is common knowledge that all of these writers exercised a high degree of sexual restraint in their youth—not, by the way, from any lack of interest in the erotic—and in this way they enhanced their talents in other areas. They became builders of bridges or aqueducts to heaven, so to speak, with the result that not even in heaven could an honorable maiden be secure from the intrusive desire of men. For it is clearly absurd to say that sublimated desire is no longer desire. And once such bridges have been built they can be crossed in both directions.

Consider the story "Alkmene," for example; it recounts the process by which an angelic being is drawn by a man's erotic fantasies and megalomaniacal self-regard into a physical body and thereby crippled. To see this, however, one must be willing to entertain two hypotheses not widely held today. The first is that no matter how great their differences in wordly power and position, human beings share a common inner world that differs from person to person only in the extent to which each has access to it. The second hypothesis concerns time as the medium of revelation, by which I mean that as time proceeds, it transforms invisible into visible reality. The poet Sophus Claussen, to take a specific case, clearly lived in expectation of the day when the woman who for so long had lived in his dreams and his hopes would appear in the visible world, "perhaps merrily riding down through Ermelund." From the moment in his youth when he broke off his engagement to his pale fiancée because he had fallen in love with God's mother and wished to build cathedrals, he had been looking for her everywhere—not in the antiquated figure of the sorrowful and merciful mother, but as "chimera, sibyl, the image of my desire."

It is easy to state what is unique about Pellegrina but difficult to say what this uniqueness means. As she says to Niccolo in "Echoes" when he asks her if she is an angel, "I was an angel once . . . but I let my flight feathers wither and fall off." Of course she speaks like this for the benefit of children and childlike souls like Niccolo, but even when this is not the case these two texts contain passages where the contradictions are even stronger and more mythologically grandiose.

In a somewhat detailed yet still simplified form, Pellegrina's biography is as follows. Nothing is known of her youth except that her father was a baker. At sixteen, while singing in a theater in Venice, she was discovered by a fabulously wealthy Jew, Marcus Cocozza. Henceforth he devoted himself to her, forever circling around her like the moon around the earth, because her song could raise her listeners "higher than the moon" and enable them to move with complete security "in life's depths and mysteries." From their first meeting he loved her with the inextinguishable love with which a person can love himself, his own goodness and intelligence, his own unfathomable and incomparable greatness. And so with his help she became a star of the first order in the musical heavens; the other women singers in the theater called her Lucifera, because she acted like a devil toward them and would tolerate no competition. But the poor in the galleries worshiped her "as a Madonna of their own, and the manifestation upon the earth of God in His heaven." She reciprocated their love with a passion "which was as mild as the Virgin Mary's love for humanity." Or as she said to Marcus: "Let me be a divinity worshiping the sinners."

During the fire at the opera house of Milan, she is struck on stage by a burning beam but is rescued from the building with her hair and clothes in flames. When she later regains consciousness, she finds she has lost her voice, which here is also called her soul. In light of her loss she makes a decision: though unable to die in fact, she will act as if she had died, and she begs Marcus to assume the unusually heavy responsibility of helping her realize her project:

> Pellegrina is dead. Nobody, nobody must ever be Pellegrina again. To have her once more upon the stage of life, of this hard world, and to have such awful things happen

to her as happen to people on the earth—no, that must not be thought of. No human being could stand the thought. Now, will you promise me that, first of all? (P. 344)

In the garden a stone is erected for her with her name and dates, and beneath are the words: *By the grace of God.* At one point in the story she says to her lover, Lincoln, that she does indeed have a heart but that it lies buried in the garden of a villa near Milan.

She and Marcus close the book on her past life and plot her future course. "From heaven a star has fallen," she quotes to him. "I will not be one person again, Marcus, I will be always many persons from now. Never again will I have my heart and my whole life bound up with one woman, to suffer so much." She then sets out on the voyage from identity to identity that comprises the greater part of "The Dreamers" and lasts until her second death thirteen years later.

In these various female figures she lives a number of lives, something a reader attentive to chronology will find improbable, for there is not enough time for all of them in the space of thirteen years, certainly not if the lives are ordered consecutively. If these hasty sketches of female destiny are taken as standing for entire lifetimes, incarnations, we would have to locate the beginning of Pellegrina's alternating phases of happiness and unhappiness far back in history. But here the author maintains a deliberate ambiguity of the kind obtained between ontogeny and phylogeny, where the present time of the child reflects the history of the race and the race in each individual produces an abbreviated history of itself. What these female figures have in common is an abundance of life that makes them the center of attention everywhere and irresistibly attractive to men. For they are always involved with men, to whom in varying degrees they give themselves—like the pious widow who goes no farther than spiritual understanding and friendship, like the revolutionary milliner who gives herself to no man in particular but rather to the French Revolution in general, like the

Roman prostitute who apparently exercises no restraint or scruple. And yet all of these women remain equally unobtainable. For each of them there is a line beyond which she mockingly, deceptively, and inexplicably slips away and disappears. Not only can they not really be owned, they cannot even be understood. The men who they have loved are left with intense and confused feelings of longing, as if the very core of their being or its finest quality had appeared to them in the form of a woman who had merrily made love to them, tweaked them by the nose, and then vanished.

More than twenty years after "The Dreamers," Karen Blixen added a new chapter to Pellegrina's story with the tale "Echoes." In it she interrupts her character's flight from her lost identity by a meeting that has the effect of temporarily canceling her self-imposed amnesia. The meeting is situated in the time between her flight from Lincoln Forsner in Rome and her second death. There is even less room in her fictional chronology for this episode than for the others.

In the story, Pellegrina comes to small mountain village near Rome, and entering a church she happens to hear the Magnificat, Mary's hymn of praise—"from henceforth all generations shall call me blessed"—being sung so beautifully by a young boy that she falls to her knees on the spot, overwhelmed, weeping, laughing: " 'O Sweet. Sweetness of life! Welcome back.' Her body fell from her like a cloak as her soul rose into heaven on the tones resounding around her. For the voice that was singing was one she knew well. It was the voice of the young Pellegrina Leoni."

She rents a small apartment in the town so as to be able to become the boy's singing teacher. She hopes to develop his voice to the same fullness and power as her voice had at its best. While thus engaged, she is struck by an odd thought. She begins thinking about the Phoenix, the bird that burns itself in its nest in order to allow its single egg to be hatched by the flames, for there must never be more than one Phoenix in the world at a time.

Twelve years ago this boy was still a baby. He may well have been born at the hour of the Opera fire in Milan. Was, then, that fire in reality kindled by my own hand? And was the flaming death of the old Phoenix and the radiant death of the young bird but one and the same thing?

Her thoughts also move toward the future, to the resurrection she is attempting to bring about.

Christ Himself, she remembered, when risen from His grave had dwelt for only forty days among His disciples, yet upon these forty days the whole world had built up its creed. Her audience, her gilt boxes and her pits and her beloved galleries would hear Pellegrina sing once more, would bear witness, with its own ears, to a miracle, and would build upon it its hope of salvation. Would she herself, she wondered, on the first night of Emanuele's appearance, be hidden away in the gallery, an old unknown woman in a black shawl, the corpse in the grave witnessing its own resurrection? (P. 170)

Her relationship with Emanuele, however, develops far differently than planned. She throws herself into it with all the accumulated energy of a passion that has lain dormant for thirteen years. "I have got my talons in him. He will not escape me," she thinks, and with a smile she remembers Marcus's remark to her when he compared her to God's creature, Leviathan, in the Book of Job: "Her heart is as firm as a stone, aye, like the nether millstone. Out of her nostrils goeth fire, and a flame goeth out of her mouth." All at once the possibility that her life might become a success after all—that it might become, in an earthly sense, whole—stirs her to life. The thought that her voice and soul, lost after the fire, might still exist in the world and that they might, by some miracle, rise from the dead and launch a new gospel, restores her adamant strength. Not that she has become any wiser through her misfortunes, for the point of the intended miracle, in her view, is precisely to prove that her former passionate self-preoccupation was necessary and fully justified. Soon the boy is ensnared by her tenderness, her wisdom, and her fierce will to dominate every "young person of the male sex." But in the midst of his enchantment he wakes up, frightened by her wild attitudes and her witchlike hints of being on friendly terms with the devil, with whom she even claims to have exchanged gifts. Certainly this sort of talk may be considered reckless and cruel when directed at a boy freshly plucked from the choir of a village church. But to make matter's worse, the boy finds that as his voice improves under her instruction, it becomes strange to him. He does not recognize it when he sings; it is as if he hears it coming from outside of him. "The whole world sang in his voice."

At last he runs away from her, shouting that she is a witch and a vampire. When she runs after him, he throws a stone at her that cuts her on the forehead. " 'Do you know at whom you are throwing stones?' she calls back. 'A thousand men, a Pope, an Emperor, Princes, gondolieri and beggars, if I but lift my voice, will be here to avenge me on you, you fool.' "

There is something outrageous, something wildly disproportionate, in the things Pellegrina thinks and in the things she says to Niccolo and Emanuele. Apparently she believes that if the boy's voice could be developed to its full capacity, it would not be really his voice but hers that was singing. Or that if he shouts insults and throws stones at her it is because he mistakenly believes that he is throwing stones at a strange, alluring, and mysterious woman, a daughter of the Erlkönig, while in reality she is, with the devil as her closest confidant, the Blessed Virgin; all she would need to do is openly declare her identity to have all people—ten thousand soldiers, mighty emperors, the pope himself—rush to her defense. Here the implication is apparently not that her one human life is more than a single life, but rather that her many lives, in the final analysis, form only one.

Through the many remarkable things she says about herself runs a unifying thought, a conviction: that what happens to Pellegrina does so by virtue of a necessity that does not originate with her. Events befall her. So that even as an outcast she is still the chosen one, blessed among women. This brings to light one of the fundamental but unstated convictions in Karen Blixen's works, which is that women are not responsible in the same way as men; they are judged by different criteria. They are beings of greater depth than men, but since they occupy an exposed position in the male world, silence becomes their second nature. All of this is implicit in Pellegrina's thoughts about the Phoenix—that is, that perhaps the fire that destroyed her was in fact ignited by her hand. For not only was that fire a very peculiar one, she now understands that neither was it an ordinary personal misfortune. Rather, it was like the death in a sacred ritual that only momentarily obscures the truth and the justice about to be revealed.

Fires of the sort that struck Pellegrina have flared up in literature many times, both before and since, around writers who have been more or less (usually less) successful in saving themselves without the rest of the world being aware of the nature of their peril. One can read about such fires in the writings of Goethe, Rousseau, Rimbaud, Sophus Claussen, and Frank Jæger. And if we look carefully, we can find an advance warning of the fire in "The Dreamers." In Pellegrina's total concentration on the voice that gives her her social identity, and in the equally total subjugation of her erotic drive to the service of her voice, we can find the spark that caused the fire to break out. In esoteric lore one finds the notion of the kundalini power, an energy that in its normal state lies coiled at the base of the spine but that can burn its way upward, releasing destructive flames into the ether body and its network of centers (chakras), which otherwise forms a kind of protective wall between the body and the soul. If such an event occurs prematurely in a person's development, it can cut off the connection to the higher self.

In a sonnet, *The Prophet of Sjælland*, Frank Jæger has depicted a moment in which one of these totally unpredictable events occurs. Meanwhile, the trees go on budding as dutifully and unconcernedly as they do every year.

> *I meant to rest my neck upon a star*
> *and let myself be lifted by the winds*
> *like the sun and the other minor prophets.*
> *I was betrayed and cast down in the night.*
>
> *I screamed, Oh I screamed, and my breath*
> *and voice shot like flames from my lips*
> *while time slid coldly past me. My stars*
> *saw my downfall and gave witness forever.*
>
> *But the past rose from the dark abyss.*
> *A person stood up and lighted the fire*
> *And the sea's lips laughed, and the woods raised*
>
> *its green tent as before. Then your air*
> *O earth, burned marvellously around me.*
> *And, betrayed, I knew that I had come home.*

The story "Echoes" is told entirely from Pellegrina's point of view; her thoughts and hopes so permeate the action that at first they are indistinguishable from it. But if one forgets them for a moment and tries to see how things conceivably might look to Emanuele, one discovers that the boy has very little to work with. All he can see is that for some unknown reason a bizarre, overbearing, and incomprehensible lady has picked him out in order to badger and love him into becoming an artist, which may be a gift beyond his greatest dreams, perhaps, but a strange and intimidating one as well. And if one tries to imagine the eventual outcome of Pellegrina's miraculous project, which is that fifteen or sixteen years after her death her beloved galleries will be able to experience her resurrection on stage in the body of a young male singer, it is clear that it is a plan that makes more sense in her mind than if one tries to see it from the standpoint of the audience. Only she and her friend Marcus would really be able to grasp what was taking place.

Throughout this dark and mysterious story one can glimpse a different conflict than its ostensible one. Pellegrina dreams of recovering the unity of her being, of bringing her past and her present together, through one great artistic exploit. Earlier in her life she was struck by a misfortune against which her entire self rises up in protest: she suffered the loss of her soul, which she mourns as she would a kidnapped daughter. This loss has imposed a dualism on her that is foreign to her and that she is now struggling to overcome. She exemplifies a kind of monism, not so much a philosophical monism as one of the will—along the lines of what Kasparson tried to accomplish in his disguise as a cardinal, or Cardinal Salviati in the secret room he built for himself inside the Catholic church.

On the perennially debated topic of monism versus dualism, Karen Blixen wrote to me in a letter from May 1954:

And about my relationship to nature: I cannot see that there is any line separating nature and human beings. On the other hand, I am not so stupid as to not recognize that others do see such a line, or to know what they mean by it. I would say to Clara, whenever we would discuss these sorts of problems, that I would like to believe that she, for example, had an immortal soul, but that I personally doubted that I had one. I would prefer the fate of Shelley's Adonis: "He is made one with nature." You say that nature is without memory—but I have often wished that I had a memory like a tree that carries each of its annual rings imprinted upon its being. I cannot, in the final analysis, really grasp any kind of "dualism."

# At Rungstedlund

*To Frans Lasson*

## 1.

For many years I have felt I ought to tell the story of my relationship with Karen Blixen. During the last ten years I have been requested to do so several times, and now, as Karen Blixen's fame increases year by year, others have even begun to tell the story of our friendship as they imagine she must have experienced it. But since that is utterly impossible for them, the story becomes very distorted. More than the numerous requests, it is these caricatures that have prompted me, as so many times previously, to try to tell the story myself.

There were a number of reasons why in the past I would always stop at the beginning or halfway through, the chief one being that, unfortunately, it is not possible to make this story plausible, that is, believable in present-day psychological terms. Second, it is inevitable that certain matters be included that lend themselves to facile misinterpretations and consequently ought not to be included if I were to follow the old rule and "speak only the good about the dead"—good taken here in its sense of the commonly praised virtues. Finally, the delightful thing about meeting Karen Blixen was that she instantly transformed a professor's visit to a famous author into a personal relationship. It was never as if I were sitting at the master's feet, transcribing words of wisdom. But even less was it the case of a meeting between two people of equal strength or wisdom. Since I have to include myself as part of this story, it will be as someone who for a long time was up against forces of stunning superiority. This of course does not mean that I have to tell ghost stories or demean Karen Blixen in the eyes of the moralists or, perhaps least of all, portray myself as a comic figure.

But why even make the attempt? Because Karen Blixen was a disruptive event in Danish and the Western world's modern culture, one that broke in and struck at its foundation to a degree that will become clear only in the future. I would like to participate in hastening the process. And because personal relationships, despite all of the great and glamorous publicity around her, were the medium through which she most genuinely and unreservedly revealed herself.

The occasion of our meeting was the two lectures "Karen Blixen and Marionettes" that I gave on the radio in 1951 and were published in the form of a very small book the following year by Wivel's publishing house. This led to several charming literary teas at Rungstedlund. Since, before meeting her, I had feared that I might have to walk around on spiritual stilts, be witty, and call her Baroness, I was relieved to find that she was very unaffected and was all the happier with people the more openly they stated their opinions. Of course, it helped that my frankness stemmed from my great admiration for her, but it is nevertheless true that things at Rungstedlund were much different and simpler than rumor would have had it. Not until the beginning of the summer of 1953 did our relationship involve anything more than literary conversation.

Then one day in June we spent the day together, and for the first time she deployed for me the whole range of her funny stories, sibylline words of wisdom, lofty proclamations, and angry condemnations of modern ills, these latter ranging from Hans Brix's books to the traffic on Strandvej. The visit filled me with so much excitement and so many expectations that when I got home I sat down and wrote her a long letter in rhyming verse.*

The decisive turning point in our relationship occurred one Sunday afternoon in July, when we were sitting alone on her veranda. She said she wanted to tell me something in complete confidentiality. She then told me the story of her illness, and I repeat it here from memory, without consulting the information that has been published about it in recent years. In 1915, she said, she traveled from Kenya to Paris to be treated for the syphilitic infection she had incurred in her marriage. The doctor who examined her asked her in astonishment how long she had been sick. When she told him it was about two years, he said, shaking his head: "My dear child, you must have lived the life of a cavalry officer. The disease is already in its third stage." He advised her to go to Copenhagen, where she could receive a treatment that at the time was the best in Europe. She followed his advice and was treated by Professor Rasch in the Rigshospital. To her family she pretended to have caught a tropical infection, and she made arrangements at the hospital to be placed in a ward that would that would not reveal the true nature of her illness. She felt that her honor and reputation were at stake, and her husband's as well. If the truth were known, they would both become objects of scandal and placed in an indefensible position. But as she lay there, uprooted from her African world, confined to the moralistic Denmark from which she had fled, forced to keep secret the condition that constantly occupied her thoughts, she felt that she was about

*In this rhyming letter, I identified myself with the Danish poet Jens Baggesen, about whom I was writing a book at the time. I resurrected this very polemical and consequently much-hated man and brought him back to Rungstedlund in my person. Since Baggesen was a poet who because of personal problems had been unable to complete his most ambitious literary project, the poem "Thora," and since he had received much help in his youth from the poet Johannes Ewald, the former owner of Karen Blixen's house, I fantasized in my poem that she would be able to solve both Baggesen's and my problems at the same time.

to die from loneliness. But then all at once in her solitary sickroom she received a visit from a being who did not find her situation so impossible. In fact, he felt that there was something "fun" about it. "And from that day," she ended her account, "I have called the Devil my best friend. He gave me the gift of being able to transform everything that happened to me from then on into a story."

This story, so clear in all of its details, burned itself into my consciousness—or perhaps it would be more correct to say that it burned itself half into and half out of my consciousness. With it begins my personal relationship to Karen Blixen. That Sunday afternoon, with the sun shining on Rungsted's summer lawn and the shouts of the swimmers mixing with the noise of the traffic on the shore highway, I unhesitatingly chose what I considered to be the better way: to accompany Karen Blixen into the shadows and the uncanny riddles of her sickroom. That day drew a line through my life. Before it was a long stretch of time in which my hopes steadily diminished; after it, a time in which I experienced a hope I could rely on. If it is true, as some have said, that I was seduced by Karen Blixen, it must also be said that I wanted to be seduced, I would not let go of her, and I have never regretted it. Her world was different from what I had reluctantly let myself imagine. It was not pleasant, I knew that, but there was something to it. No entirely sound person, secure in his or her salvation, could have given me what she gave.

I could only make sense of what she told me by connecting it to her many years of suffering from her painful disease and her insecurity about the future. The disease, for that matter, could still have been at work in her, for she said to me, "It is still possible that I might go insane, and if that happens you must be a true friend and frankly tell me so." Yes, I answered, shaken, yes, without really being able to imagine such a situation. The Devil, on the other hand, was a gentleman I knew nothing about. Of course I had heard nasty rumors about him, but as a good Danish academic I did not believe in God, let alone the Devil. And yet here he was, not as a roaring lion or with thundering hooves but as a slight thickening of the light in a lonely hospital room, a whispered message, almost a whim or a way out of an otherwise closed situation: to hide her real condition behind a story about a tropical disease allowed her to maintain her mask among "respectable" people, but with the result that her life would divide into two parts, a public one and a secret one. He could join the two by making her into a storyteller. And indeed a story did come out of it, a good, strong, bitter story, but as I imagined my way into it, I found that its psychologically interesting and menacing aspects militated against my sympathy, and it became harder for me to keep her silhouette in focus as she sat facing me, thin and ravaged, with so much suffering stored up in her.

Even taking into account that the Devil does not exist, I found a pact with the mere fantasy of him sufficiently scandalous to make me want to take to my heels. But she sat there with an air that implied that her improper story did not in any way excuse her listener from behaving properly. And so I behaved myself, in deference to her greater worldly experience.

Later I read Thorkild Bjørnvig's account of the same scene and the same story, and again, very recently, Jørgen Kalckar's account in his *Memories of Karen Blixen*. It has long been clear to me that we all experienced that private conversation as more confidential than it really was, or as confidential in a different way than it was. It was more a kind of rite of acceptance Karen Blixen used when she wanted to bring a person into her life. All of us felt that to be admitted into her confidence was the central and most moving aspect of the situation, and we grasped far less clearly the several distances her story also established between narrator and listener. Kalckar gives a beautiful account of *his* evening when "Karen Blixen suddenly took off her mask— or at least that mask." He shows how genuinely moved he was, yet without hiding the alert attentiveness with which he took note of all the odd twists and turns in the situation:

Her icy mood of sinister gloom would have made me want to run away from her as quickly as from a witch, had not my compassion, faced with a sorrow of the magnitude she revealed, proved stronger than my fear. Unable to find words of consolation, I embraced her in silence and for a brief moment her head rested upon my shoulder. Then, quick as lightning, her mood changed, we drank a glass of wine, and she was smiling and cheerful when I said goodbye.

I include Kalckar's account here because it shows the same emotional swings and describes them in almost the same terms as mine, although I wrote mine before I read his. Both of us politely and deferentially saw the situation as one in which she, as the main character, needed to confide in an understanding friend. The bizarre thought that perhaps we were the main characters and that she was using the occasion to tell us things for reasons we ignored was one we did not allow ourselves to think. Kalckar, however, is not totally blind to that possibility. He writes somewhere that one day she told him she wanted to be on a first-name basis with him, and that this phase in their relationship ought to be initiated by a mixing of their blood. "By mixing blood with a *witch*," he writes, "I would make a pact with the deep and hidden powers in life." As he jokingly tried to ward her off by various excuses, "I felt," he writes, "that she was observing me with a mixture of expectation and scorn, and there ensued a long silence."

For my part, I was not able to go along with all of her notions as gently and quietly as Kalckar.

On my way back to Lund, where I was living at the time, I tried to think through what she had told me, but without success. Finally I turned to Søren Kierkegaard and his psychological reflections on theology. Her situation had to be the one in *Fear and Trembling* that he designates as the "demonic paradox," the one to which people are exposed who "through nature or historical circumstance" are placed outside of the general situation. They cannot be saved through inclusion in society and so are either "damned in the demonic paradox or saved in the divine one." Both paradoxes imply that the individual as the individual raises himself above the general situation by means of an absolute relation to the absolute.

I put this in a letter to her, at no risk to myself, for one could bore her but one could not insult her, least of all by burrowing into her perverse riddles. A short while later came her interested reply:

Last Sunday when you asked me, à propos my "story", the real reason why I turned to, or thought that I had to turn to, the "Devil", I was not able to answer you, but could only say—as Goldschmidt writes somewhere in his memoirs— that so it was. And now you yourself, in your letter, supply the answer. You write about the "demonic paradox"—"when the individual as the individual wants to raise himself above the general situation, in other words, on his own assert the validity of his personality though he secretly stands outside the community and its value judgements." What you—and S. K.—here express in theory, I know through experience, and can therefore say that when a person chooses not to have something seen as a misfortune or a loss which otherwise the community would view as such—then His Satanic Majesty is an excellent, an irreplaceable ally—also because he is a joker and can laugh—"guffaw" would not be the pretty or appropriate term here. Naturally he sets certain conditions for his assistance. And it is, I guess, from around the time when I called upon him most urgently that I stopped recognizing or taking physical pain into account.

Here is another quotation—in explanation of the things I told you about—that your essay (or rather Brandt's book, which I read because of your essay) has given me. Goldschmidt writes that, "when Møller collapsed in his battle with S. K., it was, at its deepest level, because K. stood in a more beautiful, purer, higher relationship to woman." I must be allowed to use this to explain that if women can laugh at men, the reason is, "at its deepest level—(see

Goethe's Faust and Mephistopholes, and Thomas Mann's
Dr. Faustus and his Devil) because they stand in a more
gracious and dignified relation to the Devil."

(Generally speaking: whenever the highest representatives of light and darkness enter consciousness as a *he*,
through whom women are given access to erotic life, we
get the Virgin Mary and the Witch. If we still worshipped
the moon as a goddess, a young man could aspire to become Endymion—in the same way as I believe that young
Vikings used to entertain a very gracious and noble relationship with the goddess Ran.) But I can tell you something else about the one whom poor Clara has to hear me
call my best friend. For a year I have had to bear the weight
of something I felt to be a great sorrow, but which, in the
general opinion is no sorrow at all. No one, in any case,
with whom I have tried to discuss it has been willing or
able to recognize it as such. Here my formerly faithful ally
cannot help me. For the sake of our old friendship, he
grants me a certain melancholy—as well as a slightly
impatient—sympathy. But he flatly states that he cannot
help me, and when I ask him: "Who can?" he answers: "I
do not know." There is something truly sad about that!

Aside from its characteristic ending—it takes off from
the earth, gives a cry, and then turns its back on its recipient,
or is it just the reverse, that the recipient is precisely the
one who can do something that even the Devil cannot
accomplish?—the letter did not enlighten me much. While
her disease could hardly be held against her, it was equally
true that the kind of pious conventionality that would have
been scandalized by it and condemned it could not be called
God or the highest representative of the light, and so could
not have necessitated such a risky conspiracy. But as her
subsequent remarks suggest, she did not consider this unique
and dangerous relationship to be so unique after all, but
rather a human experience that women could deal with better than men.

She talked to me about these things with such confident

assurance that it did not occur to me to doubt their reality, but I had no idea where that reality was; least of all could I resolve the contradiction that on the one hand His Satanic Majesty was visibly present at Rungstedlund, ready at the drop of a hat to provide good advice, and that on the other he was simultaneously busy everywhere else. I had, however, exhausted my Kierkegaardian categories, so our theological conversation ended for the time being.

It may seem that our conversation was obscure and crazy, a kind of folie à deux, but it did not seem so to me. Though very uncertain as to where I was heading, I had found an opening where I had not dreamed of finding one. In the seamless wall of contemporary academic concepts that encircled me like an unshakable depression, I had found a spot that yielded to the touch. It could not really be called a clearing, I suppose, but it contained so much intricate and learned mythology it could not really be called darkness either.

## 2.

While Karen Blixen was self-confidently proclaiming notions so bizarre that one would have had to consult Johann Sprenger's *The Hammer of Witches* for commentary, I adopted a cautious, tentative attitude. I knew that she could suddenly throw off her mystical airs and in the blink of an eye become entirely present, contemporary. Indeed, that was the reason why I was sitting and listening to her in the first place.

One such transformation had occurred before I met her in the spring of 1951, at a time when I had arrived at a low point in my life. Well launched into an academic career devoted to the study of literature, I had reached the conclusion that none of it was worth the effort. The part of myself that could not conform to my seemingly orderly existence was laying hold of all of my energy. Looking about me with eyes opened by my inner conflict, I saw everything natural and logical and entitled to exist in the process of being stifled—in education, in cultural life, in politics. I had come to the standpoint that an entire generation of youth in the Western world was to reach twenty years later. I sided with North Korea against South Korea, with the Communists against the capitalists, with the children against the adults, and I found in the writings of Wilhelm Reich the ideal nucleus around which all of my anger and impatient opposition could crystallize. But in the meantime, I dutifully continued to go back and forth to the University of Lund to teach literature courses that no longer concerned me. In the spring semester I was scheduled to teach a course on the Danish short story. Then it was that Karen Blixen's writings came my way and sliced into my acute misery.

What she had written in her early marionette comedy about people acting in conflict with their desires and thus confusing nature's thoughts was not only what I was thinking myself, but even more was what I was doing and could find no way of not doing. Here at least the problem was recognized, if not solved. But when the same idea returns fifteen years later in her story about Alkmene, the beautiful child whose education kills her, it has become an artistic vision of a quiet, almost inconceivably destructive domestic process in which the entire history of the culture was implicated. The grace and power wasted by the enchanting girl in her Lutheran stepparents' home can be measured only by a standard drawn from the dawn of time. The qualities Alkmene loses are the ones humanity lost at the Fall, as recorded in Genesis. With their morality and honest fidelity to the curse uttered at the moment of expulsion from paradise, her good stepparents annihilate her. The instant I discovered this, by holding Kleist's marionette dialogue up to Karen Blixen's novella, something happened in me. In the past, the words morality and piety had always been synonymous for me, raised as I had been according to Olfert Ricard's principles, but I now saw them part company and become each other's opposites. By a complicated literary maneuver I detached myself from myself and in that instant was granted access to a large portion of my unconscious. I could now take the instincts, hunches, and recognitions that were part of the fabric of my life but excluded from academia and look at them from a higher standpoint. It was a great relief. Throughout Blixen's work I now sensed a piety for an almost angelic natural instinct in human beings, an original clarity of vision that morality and education did everything in their power to eliminate and pervert. Hereafter I could take *marionette* to designate the noble few, those who had retained the instinctive wisdom of nature but who, as artists or priests, had to pay for their dreaming, their solitary knowledge, with lives spent outside the community in whose service they were working in the fallen world.

That this was, in more than one respect, an untenable and narrow interpretation will become abundantly clear from the sequel, so I will refrain from self-criticism here. It remains true, of course, that such a view does occupy a prominent place in Karen Blixen's works, but it is also true that it is held in check by other forces I could not see at the time. This is hardly to be wondered at, all the less so in that untenable theories can be productive, as this one was throughout the nineteenth century in its various guises of Romanticism, naturalistic radicalism, and psychoanalysis. These ideas have never been revoked and continue to be active in the present day. They retain their force because they touch on something basic and promote progress. They raise the life of the body into consciousness and thereby transform themselves from ideas into an irreversible condition. When above and below and the conscious and the unconscious join together, a role is created, a provisional identity connected to a force field in which mighty energies and visions circulate.

For me, this new understanding of Karen Blixen's writings meant that the two different parts of myself—the desiring part and the reasoning part—came together again, to a certain extent at least. I wrote my doctoral thesis on Kierkegaard's novels in the light of Karen Blixen's works—a fact, as indicated above, not without historical significance. But while I was writing, I discovered that the greater the area of life to which I applied the marionette philosophy, the more nebulous it became. I could think in its terms and find its presence everywhere in prescientific times, but at no point could I anchor it to the sort of modern science that I was obliged to regard as providing the truth about things. And so I incorporated into my book a melancholy ambiguity concerning art and science. I saw art as a kind of dreaming spirit of wisdom that, by conceptually simplifying experiences and events and by providing ingenious formulas for interpreting life and articulating morality, makes life possible and allows it perpetually to hover above the humanly alien, purposelessly fermenting matter that science seeks to chart.

## 3.

With this philosophy as flimsy ballast I arrived at Rungstedlund. My philosophy quickly proved to be inadequate, however, for whatever else was implied by her disturbing talk about the Devil, it meant having a body and yet not having one; it meant being visibly present in space among people and yet not being there. It was, in its turned-around way, realistic. Thus I already needed to revise my theories, but for the moment I was unable to do so. The personal element in our relationship became so important that for a long time it preoccupied my thoughts and blocked my view.

To meet and be with the person who for many years had occupied my thoughts and changed my life both lifted my spirits and filled me with expectations in a way that I could hardly understand. It induced feelings in me that were, and still are, almost impossible to express. I was caught up in an intoxication of identification beyond anything I had thought possible, so that taking my solitary walks around Lund I felt that she was smiling with the muscles in my face and speaking with my vocal cords. I wondered if the fact that my mother was born the day after Karen Blixen might in some strange way mean something. They could almost be twin sisters. I recalled stories about people who had had two mothers—Oedipus, for example, and Leonardo; my old friend Baggesen had written something along these lines in his "Thora." I imagined that Karen Blixen was going to solve my problems, which they needed, and that I, however unlikely it may now seem, was going to solve hers and eliminate that other friendship of hers of which I strongly disapproved. For about one thing I was never mistaken: in the midst of her magnificently accomplished life there was a poverty, a hopelessness, an emptiness that ought not to have been there. At night I dreamed of her as a poor concierge seated at the entrance to her own sparkling fairy tale castle. The dream concurred with what she had once said about herself, that she had died a long time ago; but this was something that my waking mind could not understand. In the confused and euphoric mood of mystery that she awakened in me were many conflicting feelings: pride at knowing her, commitment, devotion, expectancy, and a clear awareness that in many ways I was the stronger of us two. In the ordinary sense of the term I derived no advantage from knowing her. I did not want to become a new member of the "court at Rungstedlund." But the unthinkable aspects of her held me and enchanted me. The iron discipline with which, despite her debilitating disease and advancing age, she pursued her goal, maintained her standards, and continued to transform herself by some hidden law—all of this without the least anchor or support in the world around her, moving ever farther away from well-traveled areas—filled me with an admiration in which there was also some fear: this is happening here and now, this is not possible, but it is happening, and no one else sees it. She put me in mind of Grundtvig's Easter lily:

> *I only give joy*
> *To the loving eye*

*That can understand*

*What I signify*

She signified in any event the presence of other forces and the possibility of living outside the cosmology of the modern world. This in itself made her a messenger. Whatever more specific meaning she might have had I could not for the moment determine. This might sound cold on my part, as if I were puzzling over her as over a difficult riddle, which in a way I was, but only in the sense that I had begun to see in her the riddle of my own self. However implausible it may seem, I felt in looking at her like I was looking at my own soul.

It did not inhibit our relationship that in addition to being a person she also functioned for me as a sign; on the contrary, she was scrupulous in carrying out that function. In the same way as she had let her letter about Kierkegaard trail off in an obscure mumbling, she would scatter vague hints through our conversations about things about which I knew nothing that might happen in the future if everything went well. "It was oddly appropriate," she wrote to me once when I had given her a number of my writings: the manuscript of my doctoral dissertation, notes on Baggesen's "Thora," my rhyming letter, my remarks about her Albondocani project. This entire stack of paper was "oddly appropriate." I was starting to think that I fit just as surprisingly into her life as she did in mine. Later on I have often wondered why I did not routinely ask her what these coincidences were supposed to mean, but at the time my imagination seized upon her hints as upon so many promises of future blessings. What is said of certain works, that they are like mirrors and reflect only the viewer, applies much more so to hints, for here the listener has to finish all the sentences himself.

I did not know how much weight to give to my speculations and guesses until the spring of 1953, when a certain *An Evening in the Cholera-Year* was published by someone writing under the pseudonym Alexis Hareng. Tage Skou-

Hansen, the editor of the journal *Vindrosen*, called me up and asked if I would review the book, which many people thought had been written by Blixen. The book was turning into a literary affair because it was being published under the same sort of camouflage system that she had used with several of her books. *Seven Gothic Tales* and *The Angelic Avengers* were of course both published pseudonymously, and in the case of the latter, Karen Blixen had publicly defended an author's right to keep her identity hidden. "I have read *The Angelic Avengers*," she had written, "and I can definitely assure you that were I the author I would under no circumstances acknowledge it." Hans Brix was entirely in the right to state that Karen Blixen's notion of pseudonymity as an assumed mask that the world was obliged to respect was contrary to all literary usage. All the aliases of interest to scholars eventually get uncovered and neatly printed in literary lexicons. But what Brix could not grasp or accept was that Karen Blixen as a person was always pseudonymous in varying degrees, that she always wanted to be suspected behind her texts but under no circumstances caught. And it was these sublime conditions that I, as one who was aware of her desires, now wanted to satisfy.

With great impatience I waited for the book, which apparently was the talk of Copenhagen but which no one in Lund knew anything about. Finally it arrived, and after reading one page I fell abruptly back down to earth and announced sadly to my wife: This is not by Karen Blixen. During the following days, however, all of the hints and half promises of recent years gathered around my head, all of the things that had been so strangely appropriate, and I recognized traces of them in the book. Building on these, I put together an overly ingenious interpretation of the book as an anagrammatical collaboration between the two of us, which then meant, in a way, that its true author was our impossible but nevertheless real friendship. I wrote to her in a letter, which since has disappeared, probably in the fireplace, that I found the book to be a "profound joke." Promptly I received this answer:

I have no way of knowing in this instance what you mean by "a profound joke." My own feelings in the matter are: for the author—I know who he is, but will not mention his name before it is revealed by others, as I assume it inevitably will be—that he is a guttersnipe, although unfortunately not a very witty one. I feel no moral indignation and I am willing to let him be seen for what he is. As for the publishers, I find their behavior to be a fairly nasty infringement of ordinary business ethics. They have tricked the bookstores with their impudent advertisement—and it is for the sake of the bookstores, to which after all I owe my laurel crown and toward whom I feel some obligation, that I have demanded a disclaimer. But then of course the bookstores have in turn tricked the public, which in this case does not deserve much better. I am no expert in business ethics, so I will let my attorney take care of that side of things. The remarkably petty nastiness shown by the newspapers makes me hope they will never write another article about me again—perhaps they are right that I do not really belong in "Danish cultural life." But finally—as for my friends, especially my literary friends, I am sad and disappointed that none of them reacted against a situation in which an insult to a totally innocent human being inevitably had to lead to all sorts of gossip being spread about this innocent party's history and relationships and private person. Now, however, I am going to forget the entire matter, I want nothing further to do with it.

The letter hit me like a blow. In a flash my ingenious interpretation was blown down like a house of cards, flat, gone, already impossible to remember. For several days I had been living in a state of complete unreality, but what was it but the sudden precipitate of several years of a more nebulous unreality? I felt weightless, tricked, but tricked by myself. When I visited her several days later to discuss the whole miserable business I could find no words of explanation or comfort. They were sorely needed. Despite her letter's assurance that she would now forget everything, she was in a state of nervous unrest and on the verge of making great resolutions, at which she hints in her letter, for how was she to avoid being written about in Denmark? First of all, she suggested, by withdrawing an article about the novel *The Riding Master* from *Vindrosen*. Then by ceasing to write in Danish, the language that had become contaminated for her. And finally, perhaps, by leaving the country for good and settling abroad. In this way everyone would be punished, with the exception of me. That evening, after I had told her why I had read *The Cholera-Year* as I had, she said, "It is just like in my story, 'A Consolatory Tale.'" In "A Consolatory Tale" the beggar, Fath, disguises himself to look like the prince of the country, Nazrud Din, while the prince disguises himself and goes out among his people in order to see their conditions firsthand. When the people see Fath, they feel embraced by the prince's greatness and compassion. Well, that was one way to explain my mistake. But I did not want to be excused and be allowed to go back to my old self again, now that I had seen that self in action.

Whether Kelvin Lindemann was as guilty and whether Carit Andersen's publishing house was as nasty as they both appeared when seen from Rungstedlund, I will not say; I can only see the affair from my own biased viewpoint. But my present view is that these merry gentlemen did indeed indulge themselves in a fairly coarse practical joke, all the while laying their heads in Karen Blixen's lap. She could have put a stop to their game any moment she wished—by writing a review of the book or a new essay on pseudonymity. Kierkegaard, for example, published the majority of his books under pseudonyms, but from early on he used them because they allowed him to play an internal game with positions and points of view. No one ever needed to be in doubt about who ultimately was the author. And she, too, could have exercised the right to create distances within her authorship while still preserving its wholeness. But the problem was, it seems, that she also insisted on appearing as unique and ungraspable, and she became ensnared by her own demand. It amused her to tell stories like the following, about a woman from the neighborhood around Rungsted who came to her one day because she had a husband who drank too much and was abusive. She wanted to get rid of him, if Karen Blixen could arrange it. Of course her request was turned down, but a month later a large basket of fresh asparagus arrived at Rungstedlund with the note: "To Baroness Karen Blixen." It seems that a few days previously the woman's husband had fallen down some stairs and broken his neck. On the other hand, when the writer Ole Sarvig visited her during *The Cholera-Year* episode with an article suggesting that she, the fine lady artist, had been knocked down by a ringmaster's baton from Bakkens Hvile (a popular tavern in Dyrehavsbakken amusement park), she rejected his notion out of hand. She had no idea what a ringmaster's baton was nor Bakkens Hvile, and she refused to be associated with either one.

Personally, as I mentioned above, I did not want to get out of my part of the story by having it explained away or excused. In November and December, I wrote two small things, an article and a grotesque short story based on the now-concluded affair. I began my article by referring to Brandes's essay on Goldschmidt in which he discusses the technique of allusion and hiddeness in literature, and from there I went on to try to show how *The Cholera-Year* both used and misused Blixen's mode of writing. Karen Blixen did not like the article. "But I," she wrote to me, "want no analysis of my works provoked by Alexis Hareng. Can any impostor impose a comparison? Nor is it the kind of reaction I would have expected from someone who calls himself my reader, any more than it would be the way in which I would respond if I saw an artist whom I respected being badly treated." So I put my article aside. My short story was about betrayal and self-betrayal and concerns a Baggesen-like man who has his high ambitions dashed by a rather heartless lady, a defeat that does not destroy his belief that, in spite of everything, they belong together.

If in the latter part of 1953 Karen Blixen lost patience with me, which in fact she did, it seems to me as I now look back over the letters from that time it happened in December and was caused not by my particular part in the Hareng affair but by the things I wrote afterward, especially the short story. The character I based on her is a remarkably twisted and implausible caricature, miles beneath her true level.

On the night of December 30, I stayed at Rungstedlund for an evening party that proved to be marked by painful dissonances. Alone together the following day we discussed my short story, and she said that she did not like it. Then she informed me that she had made arrangements for me to be picked up by a mutual acquaintance and driven to my parents' house in Skovshoved, where I was going to celebrate New Year's with my family. I was picked up as arranged. In the car our acquaintance went to great lengths to point out to me how much I had invested in my relationship with Karen Blixen, and concluded by asking me: "So what are you going to do now? Karen Blixen does not like losers."

I had no choice but to think that just as she had arranged the ride so had she also arranged for this annihilating remark. On the first of January, leaving the happy voices of my friends behind me, I traveled back to Lund, convinced that my relationship with Karen Blixen was over.

## 4.

The winter of 1953–54, also in respect of weather, was creakingly cold. Øresund began to freeze in January and in the beginning of February one could walk far out on the ice. In Sweden, because of its size, they are never able to sweep away all of the snow, and they let it lie until it melts.

Around the middle of February, Tage Skou-Hansen called me up about an article I had promised him on Thomas Mann. During our conversation he told me that Karen Blixen seemed very upset; she was taking walks with her dog Pasop out to the very edge of the ice, and every day at Rungstedlund they feared she might not come back. He also told me that she talked about me a great deal and kept asking why she did not hear from me. "Well, in that case," I answered, "I am not too proud." At the same time as I sent the essay about Thomas Mann's *amor fati* to Tage, I sent a copy to her along with thanks for the time I had spent with her before New Year's and for some philosophical reflections she had made to me then. Her last remark had concerned King Lear and how utterly friendless he was alone with his fool out on the heath. Since I suspected her implied meaning, I now wrote to her that if King Lear did have friends, they could hardly contradict him when he said that he was friendless, "for as to whether one is friendless or not, oneself is sole judge." Then I added:

> Sometimes I feel myself so alone in my ability to understand you that I do not even take your own views into account. This is certainly a mistaken claim for a person as unfashionably naive as I am. And yet this misinterpretation, which leaves me practically defenceless in conversation with you, in the deepest sense (I am not speaking now of my calculating attempts to save myself post mortem) springs from the same intoxicating identification with you that first opened my eyes and allowed me to see.
>
> Tage Skou-Hansen mentioned that you have been asking about me and for me. I did not expect that, but thank God, and thanks to you too. For—I cannot give rational grounds for this—in some sort of way I belong with you. This puts no pressure on you when I say this, for I am not sure myself what I mean by it.

She answered at once:

> Thank you for your letter and your essay about Thomas Mann. I have only skimmed your essay and am looking forward to re-reading it and to talking with you about it when you come here. But I wanted to thank you at once, for I have been longing to hear from you.

Let me say this while I remember it: You should not speak of your "misinterpretation" as you do. After all it took us into "A Consolatory Tale", and believe me, the story has truly been a consolation for me. The one glimpse of spirit in all this miserable honesty!

I have had, and am having, a truly terrible time because my African project has fallen through.* I had gathered all my strength for a leap and then the project was cancelled, and now I am supposed to go back to where I was before. I am, I feel, like a "betrayed" character in your story: I am bleeding to death. And in my case no one understands the extent of the pain—and yet I suppose it is better this way than doctors and a hospital!

The letter came on the morning of February 17. That afternoon the following telegram arrived: "Call Rungstedlund at once!" There were passages in my essay that she wanted to discuss before Tage printed it. The following day I traveled over to Rungstedlund. I could actually have *walked* from Sweden to Denmark, but I took a boat. The excellent and much-regretted ferry, *Malmöhus*, which at that time went back and forth between Malmö and Frihavn, was outfitted as an icebreaker and drove through the ice with splintering, crashing noise while fishermen stood calmly at their fishing holes twenty feet away. I was received at Rungstedlund as if I had accomplished a heroic voyage and not been traveling first class, and as if I, like Morten de Coninck in "The Supper at Elsinore," had come straight from hell. Recall that he says to his sister Fanny, "I have come now, as you see, because the Sound is frozen over. I can come then. That is the rule." It was a day full of happiness and homecoming and the feeling of having grown several years older. We were beginning over again on newly swept ground. The pleasures of the day extended late into the evening, for sud-

---

*At the time of the first Kikuyu uprising and political murders in Kenya, several large newspapers proposed to send Karen Blixen to Africa in the hope that she might be able to improve the situation.

denly all of the fuses in the house blew with one loud pop. At the moment I was on my way upstairs to the room above Ewald's parlor, which normally was Karen Blixen's bedroom but which she had had to vacate because of the cold. I could not even grope my way in the dark because I had never been there before, and so I stood there, nailed to the spot. I can still hear her calling down in the dark: "Clara, Clara, can't you bring a candle?" Much later, the lights came on again, but only for three seconds, after which everybody bowed to necessity and went to bed by candlelight. Thus I did not really get to see the room I was sleeping in, but I slept, for the first time at Rungstedlund, deeply and peacefully and went wandering through great pastel-colored dream landscapes. The sun woke me with its sparkling and glittering play on the windowpanes. It cast a rosy glow over two life-size cloth giraffes woven into a rug hanging on the wall at the foot of my bed. And if they were not really life-size, which most likely was the case, I enlarged them with my happiness.

Karen Blixen's interest in my essay was not unmotivated. I had written about art and coldness, about His Satanic Majesty and the modern novel, about the way in which the latter can maintain its former dimensions only by becoming a parodic repetition, a quotation, a résumé of the dying culture. These aspects of my discussion caused the ceramic gleam and the historical reminiscence in her own stories to become sharply apparent. For the sake of clarity there was even a definition of the Devil as Thomas Mann saw him: "When intellectual pride unites with psychical old age and rigidity, then the Devil appears." About the point of the essay we did not, for the moment, say anything; she went through it with me and with sublime self-confidence pointed out those places where not my words but my thought was inadequate. Before we put the manuscript away, however, she said that she had found my characterization of her and her friend "rather depressing," though otherwise she was in good spirits, as indeed she tended to be whenever anyone was on the track of her innermost identity. Several days later she wrote to me and by then was fully her old self again:

> Concerning the difference of opinion between Thomas Mann and me: probably its real cause is that Thomas Mann is German and so not to the same degree as I, who have seafaring folk in my family, *free*. Where our differences come most clearly to view is in his attitude toward, and treatment of, my (and his?) best friend. If I were to imagine that Thomas Mann and I were to be host and hostess at a party for the above-mentioned, I would first need some assurance that he would not indulge in what to me would seem like an inappropriate—and frankly speaking: mal-elevé—arrogance toward our guest. He never stops being Thomas Mann and showing the devil that he sees through him, and that is something one may not do to a guest. Especially with this guest, one must *forget oneself*.

Disregarding the seafarers, of whom Thomas Mann, who came from Lübeck and an old merchant family, probably could have found comparable examples, we find in this installment of her ongoing account of the Devil's activities the charge that Thomas Mann denies and condemns the source of his own literary talent. Artistic talent consists in the ability to halt the flow of events in oneself and to remove one's portion of the world's joys and sorrows from circulation so that it may be transformed into poetry, image, art. The Devil is a special form of spiritual metabolism. That was really what she had always been saying, translating into modern aesthetic and psychological terms an ancient and no longer tolerable symbol. When she portrayed herself as a kind of Devil's angel who was able to hand herself over in entire self-forgetfulness, she was using an image to define her literary aesthetic.

At that point our relationship had reached an equilibrium where it stayed for several years. From the time of our first meeting, even during the Hareng affair, she consulted me on literary matters and she continued to do so. Otherwise our letters were mainly concerned with my doctoral defense in the spring of 1954 and with my wife's and my move back to Denmark in 1955. She was most helpful to us; she rode around on her bicycle and inspected properties and houses and sent us written reports of her impressions. One matter that I could not mention in my letters, but which took a great deal of my time, was the preparations for her seventieth birthday on April 17, 1955. Her publisher Gyldendal naturally wanted to celebrate the day with a large party, but the idea did not appeal to her. So I mentioned to Ole Wivel that she had often expressed a desire to direct *Hamlet* in a Danish theater. I suggested that Gyldendal rent Fredriksberg Theater and Wivel was in favor of the idea, but when it came right down to it Karen Blixen was not; most likely she felt too weak. So the idea of a theatrical premiere on her birthday fell through, as did also the larger project of a festschrift which I had begun to put together with Gyldendal's support. The closer we came to her birthday, the uneasier we all became, most of all Karen Blixen. She had made no arrangements herself, and one by one we had all given up ours as inadequate. Thus as the day approached, we found we had *no* program at all. When Blixen, in growing desperation, saw that everyone knew that nothing had been arranged and was feeling sorry for her because they thought that she was unaware of the fact, under the pretext of illness she angrily left Rungstedlund and moved in with her sister in Sølvgade. By then the only way to appease her would have been to have Copenhagen illuminated, Tivoli opened, and the words KAREN BLIXEN SUPERSTAR inscribed on the night sky with fireworks. But we could not arrange that. The mood of this heartbreaking comedy reminded me of the Hareng affair, only that now there were no guilty parties to accuse—except one, of course, but it would never have occurred to Karen Blixen to think of her.

On the evening of April 17, Ole Wivel had a birthday dinner and a symposium in his home for the absent guest of honor. He had gathered some literary people who knew her personally and we took turns during dinner holding speeches about her. Several days later, when I described the evening to her, she said bitterly: "This is what Denmark can offer me, ten literary . . . whatevers, gathered around a dinner table."

During these years, she gave a new twist to her familiar habit of dropping hints and vague promises into our conversations. For some unfathomable reason, she thought up one love affair for me after the other. Now, the number of young people among our mutual acquaintances was not very large, so she did not have many women to draw on. Once she offered to pay for a two-week stay in Italy for me if I would go with a good friend's wife, whom I liked very much. Another time she prepared the situation with more forethought. A short time after I had attended a chamber concert held in her newly remodeled hayloft, she invited me to tea. When I arrived, she said that she had also invited another, more distant friend's wife, whom I will call Henriette. She asked me if I had any objections, and I said of course not. Before Henriette arrived, Karen Blixen talked enthusiastically about her lovely shoulders. Then after Henriette arrived and we were drinking tea, Karen Blixen talked about a friend of hers from Africa with whom she had gone on a safari. This friend was remarkable for her unforgettably beautiful shoulders. She remembered the sight of them from one day when her friend had wanted to bathe in the river and had had an improvised screen set up for herself. Behind these wooden slats the friend was now undressed before our eyes, garment by garment, so that it was not only her shoulders but other equally memorable parts of her that were revealed. After tea, Karen Blixen excused herself and asked me if I would show Henriette the hayloft where the concert had been held. Obedient as always, I did show her the loft, but felt very awkward and wondered whether Henriette saw through the piquant maneuver. She was an intelligent and amusing woman and I had always found it easy to talk to her, but our conversation on that occasion was stiff and cold; I had the strong feeling that Councillor Matthiesen was lurking somewhere in the half-dark of the hayloft, perhaps peering through a knothole in the paneling.

I could never take these projected love affairs seriously, for I never felt like breaking out of my marriage and into my friends'. Besides, an ability to anticipate complications was a skill I had developed early in life, and I could see that all of these "love stories" arranged by Karen Blixen were doomed to rapid and painful outcomes with harmful effects on all my other valued relationships, and I could see no point in them.

I could not be sure, but I wondered whether her behavior had something to do with yet another ambiguous episode that had happened one late winter afternoon when we were out walking on the golf course. A thin new moon like a sharp sickle stood in the northeast sky. Seeing it, she turned toward it and curtsied slowly three times. Without turning around, she stretched out her hand behind her and asked me: "Do you have a krone?" "No," I told her after I had checked, "I have only a ten-kroner bill." "That won't do, we'll have to put it off till some other time." Unfortunately, I had failed her again, but what could a coin do that a ten-kroner bill could not?

Perhaps some kind of explanation for these bizarre incidents can be found in a conversation we had one day at breakfast. This was the only time I ever said anything that provoked her into an immediate outburst of anger. We were discussing the perennial topic of her relationship with Thorkild Bjørnvig, which she said she deeply regretted. She said that he had been harmed by it—and this prompted me to say that on that score she need not worry about me. She could not harm me. I reminded her that when I was not at Rungstedlund I had another life with my wife and children that she knew nothing about. I should not have said that. Furiously, she snapped back that a person she could not hurt was a person she could not be friends with, either, and if I had another life outside of her horizon, I had best pack my bags and return home to it. Of course I did not do it, and later that day the clouds dispersed a little, but the sun did not reappear.

What I had told her was only partly true. My marriage remained unshaken and unshakable through all those years. None of the women with whom she wanted to involve me— and who certainly did not want to get mixed up with me— posed any threat to it. It was Karen Blixen who was the temptation and the danger to my marriage. She was the one who, forever unknown and the sign of some dimly glimpsed process of spiritualization, shone for me with the aura of an enigma.

# 5.

In April of 1956, a Blixen evening was held in the auditorium of the University of Oslo. With the help of the chairman of the university's student council, Kåre Lervik, who died prematurely several years later, I arranged an evening with actors, music, and a lecture by myself. My lecture was not a failure, but it was not good, either, despite the eternity I had spent in preparing it. The sources opened in me five years earlier by my reading of Blixen had dried up. Our situation had become too complex. With self-abnegating loyalty I tried to force my way by sheer willpower in the spirit of one of her own mottoes: "Remember, only hard metals ring." But this time my sword did not ring, and afterward I realized what in fact I had known in the months leading up to it: that I had finally come to an impasse.

The following day I had breakfast at the home of Erling Nielsen, the reader in Danish at the University. Alf Larsen was there too, the poet and cultural essayist who for many years was the editor and principal writer for the journal *Janus*. He was a small, sharp, cheerful man, as lively as a squirrel, brilliant. He was an anthroposophist and held forth at great length about Rudolf Steiner. With joking retorts

and smiling skepticism we listened to him without our re-
sistance making the least impression on him. He was seventy
years old at the time and for half a century had been in
opposition to everything and everybody, so he was used to
being considered a little eccentric. Lively and unconcerned,
he babbled on like a brook over all resistances—and made
an impression on us, a puzzling but definite one.

Today I would not be able to reconstruct the spiritual
short circuit that led me, upon my return to Denmark, to
summarize my conclusions from that stimulating breakfast
roughly as follows: For years I have been complaining about
my states of depression, and they are steadily growing worse.
I have reached another dead end in my life; I am thirty-four
years old; it's now or never. The salvation I had hoped for
from Karen Blixen has not occurred; depression fills my
stomach with a constant feeling of nausea. And now someone
comes along who says that there are resources in the body
to which one can gain access through artificial means. What
is the art that can seize the spirit in the farthest reaches of
the body? Yoga, of course. And so I went to the local library
and borrowed a beginner's book on yoga. "Now, what do
you want from yoga?" Karen Blixen asked me when I told
her about it. "I want to die!" I said, an answer that visibly
made an impact on her and that she stored in her memory.

It would be unreasonable of me now to be overly critical
of myself because I once tried something new. I am fortunate
that I do not have to look back with deep regret on the years
that began for me then. With the luck of a fool who casually
strolls into a mine field without having noticed the warning
signs, I managed to get through that period in one piece. It
was not my doing. With an ignorance no doubt indistinguishable from that of the official institutions of learning, but
which today I find absurd and incredible, and with an academic arrogance that was intended to annex centuries of
Eastern wisdom to its own sophomoric knowledge, I threw
myself into experiments with yoga positions and breathing
exercises. After a few days I experienced extreme discom-
fort followed by a lethargy like nothing I had known before.

This was hardly a good result, but it was, on the other hand, a result. It showed me that I could not proceed on my own. With the help of the telephone book I located a woman yoga teacher. I was her student for nine months.

After I had visited her twice I wrote to Karen Blixen about my first session:

> During our first meeting, she told me at a certain moment to sit very still and relaxed and not think about anything. Then she shook herself slightly, rolled her head and then looked down into her lap. I had almost succeeded in not thinking about anything—the seemingly impossible core of yoga—but could not actually do it because at that instant it was as if the air between us began to move with a wave-like motion, one wave after the other striking against me. "Are you noticing anything?" she asked. "No," I said, because I thought I was supposed to notice something inside, and I was feeling so distracted by these disturbances in the atmosphere. "I am streaming," she said—and no one could deny that indeed she really was streaming. I felt a bubbling and spinning inside me. This is a truth, a fact, in any case a phenomenon, whatever else it may be.

When I wrote this first report I was keeping a large ironic distance from the events, but it quickly became difficult to maintain. Obviously, the wall between me and a region of that unknown world was so thin that the exercises and my teacher's powerful presence sufficed to break through it at once. In my letter to Karen Blixen I went on to object to the use of Indian terminology in my new milieu, which I found to be a disagreeable and unnecessarily esoteric jargon, but not long afterward I began to have experiences for which there are no Western names. My teacher's presence raised the kundalini force in me; my chakras began to stir and a pulsating, seemingly electric current began to flow through my body, which it has continued to do ever since. I had visions, saw auras. Now, finally, I thought, I have something to bring to Karen Blixen that she knows nothing about. Perhaps it can bring movement to those areas in herself that she thinks are dead. And since my new experiences had made me attentive to the fact that these streams are carved or inscribed on most of the Eastern Buddha figures or meditation statues, either as ripples upon the naked limbs or as lines made by the folds of the garments, I took along a book, the next time I visited her, that would give me some sort of documentation. It was C. J. Jung and Richard Wilhelm's *The Secret of the Golden Flower*. It contains four pictures of the stages of Taoist meditation, where one can follow in detail the changes that occur in the system of energy flow during the process.

We were sitting in the green parlor. I placed the open book in front of her. With no more than a glance, she firmly pushed it away. Indian pictures and Indian modes of thought had always repelled her. She had no interest in things that smacked of spiritism. In Africa she had known a woman who was a spiritist. One night this woman had a dream in which she saw that the propellor on a certain sculpture of an airplane had been put on backward. And when they looked, they found that it was indeed backward. But what did that signify?

Her reaction did not seem to me to do the matter full justice, particularly given my expectations. Nevertheless, I had to admit to myself that the unusual experiences I was having were still rather mechanical and superficial. They were undeniably there, but they remained at the level of a curious enhancement of the world of the senses. In other words, they did not divulge their meaning. An acquaintance happened to say the appropriate word about my condition. One day when I was walking around Humlebæk with Thorkild Bjørnvig, I told him a little about my bizarre situation. "But aren't these experiences very enjoyable?" he asked. "Yes," I replied. "But not as enjoyable as one might imagine, because each time something unusual happens, up pops this little bespectacled pedant inside me and asks: 'Let's see now, what's so frightfully interesting here, let's take a closer look at it.' " Whereupon Bjørnvig gave one of his famous bellows of laughter and cried: "Yes, and I'll bet he's made of asbestos."

He was, in any case, tough. Nevertheless, in the spring of 1956 I found that certain fixed notions of mine were beginning to change. My sought-after if confusing experiences had at least shown me that one could find solutions and openings where one least expected them. They also gave me the desire to bring movement into the hard, crystalline universe of Karen Blixen's tales. There the characters are driven relentlessly forward by their passions, step by step, until suddenly they are stuck forever. And since I had no other way of gaining access to that world, I tried to sketch out a few short stories of my own that I intended to locate inside of her stories, so to speak, at those points where they yielded to pressure. The first one was never written down and I relate it here from my indistinct memory of it. The narrator is the one-hundred-year-old aunt, Medea, who sticks her head in between Taddeo and Matteo in "Tales of Two Old Gentlemen." The story is set in the seventeenth century and is about a man who has suffered defeat in a battle over a farm in northern Jutland. Forced by his enemies to flee south, he makes careful plans to surprise them and get them in his power. Filled with plans of justified revenge, he travels back north one winter day. He gets off his horse in the woods and sits down on the trunk of a fallen tree to have something to eat, but the cold makes him drowsy and he falls into a brief half-sleep. When he reopens his eyes, he sees a wolf sitting a few feet in front of him, staring at him. Frightened, he jumps to his feet and the wolf runs away; but for a second it is as if the empty form of the wolf's head remains in the cold, misty air. Suddenly all of the gluttonous and terrible features from his own face assemble themselves into the likeness of a wolf and rush to fill the empty form—then they vanish. Thoughtfully, he gets back on his horse and continues his journey at a walking pace, but a half hour later he turns his horse around and heads back south. And that is all there was to that story.

Karen Blixen's first remark about the story concerned

the horse. A horse that had been ridden a long way could not be allowed to stand tethered in the cold. Her second remark went deeper and concerned the nature of the short story. She took a piece of paper and in one unbroken line drew a pentagram: "This," she said, "is how a story looks, enclosed in itself. Nothing can be added to it and nothing taken away." But that was the central point, her concept of fate, that I did not want to accept, for I felt I personally had already gotten out of more than one story without cheating. Her third remark did not come until a few hours later, when we were out walking again on the golf course.

"That story you told me, did Thorkild Bjørnvig tell it to you and then ask you to tell it to me?"

"No, really, I thought it up myself."

My second sketch for a story was occasioned by the story "Echoes" and was an attempt to produce a male counterpart to Pellegrina. Even if she is a character living in majestic and unbreakable solitude, one could imagine another equally great but less obvious solitude, and between these two a strange, new, previously untried happiness. Thus I had Pellegrina continue on her travels from the little mountain village near Rome northward to the Abbey of St. Gallen, where she stays for a time. In the library there she meets a young Jew and begins talking to him. Their conversation turns to the topic of great cities, and as she mentions London, Rome, and St. Petersburg he proves to be fully acquainted with them and able to give her knowledgeable and interested answers. He tells her he is writing a book, and when she asks him how long he has been working on it and when he will be finished, he gives her evasive answers that somehow carry the hint of unending stretches of time, both past and future. Struck by the man's peculiarities, reminiscent of her own, she asks him—she, who can say about herself that happiness is her element—what his work in life is. He considers her question for a long time in order to gather many various aspects into one answer, and finally says: "My work has really always been to inflict pain."

As time goes on, Pellegrina begins to feel for the man

the sort of confidence that one can have for a stone or a tree to which one is indifferent and that one cannot imagine as wanting to take part in human affairs, and she tells him her story as it has been told in "The Dreamers" and "Echoes." This allows her to make the following bizarre remark: "Perhaps one day I shall have to drink your blood, but it will not help me much, for plant sap cannot help me." He gives an understanding and sorrowful reply. At this point she thinks she knows who he is, and she takes him in her arms and says: "Ahasverus, my brother." Startled, he holds her at arms' length and says: "I am not Ahasverus, the Eternal Jew. I am the disciple of whom Jesus said to Peter: And if I will that he remain until I return, what concern is that of yours?"

Though short stories are in their essence like pentagrams, I received in response to my sketch a lengthy and touching reply.

A fantasy on a story—in the form of a continuation of the story itself—from the "reviewer's" own hand is for the author a strange and witty, a most captivating and moving kind of review.

The story about the old deaf aunt and now this one about St. Gallen have both given me a great deal to think about. The only thing that I, the author/reviewer object to is a certain murkiness in the reviewer/author, and should you ever feel like expending the same rich effort on another of my stories, I would ask you to write down your fantasy as a tale. In the two cases where you have so honored me, I have had difficulty tearing myself away from your sketches, and in this there is something disturbing, almost frightening, that limits one's joy in them.

In the latter fantasy, it is the young Jew's remark: that his task is to inflict pain that confuses me.

If one takes him at his word, that he is the disciple, etc., then for me the character to whom he refers has nothing to do with inflicting pain. He is referring, of course, to John, who, in the standard interpretation is usually seen as the apostle with the least amount of pain and internal conflict and who, in his relationship to the Lord and his mother and general circle of followers, is the one least involved with the causing of pain.

And if one sees him as Pellegrina, erroneously, does: as Ahasverus—again I fail to see the logic of it. Pellegrina had heard her young friend's explanation before she tried to identify him. But for me as presumably for most people who have busied themselves with the legend, the figure of the Wandering Jew has nothing to do with inflicting pain. The greatness of the figure consists in its isolation, its remoteness from the general human condition, and to the degree that notions of pain are associated with it—as indeed they are—these must concern Ahasverus's own pain, that is, that the pain he feels in his unique situation cannot really be comprehended by others. Only a very few people would be likely to feel immediate pain at the thought of not having to die; one has the impression that even for Ahasverus his misfortune has only gradually become apparent. I have read of the Wandering Jew that in a few instances he has helped people—and that they became terrified when they discovered who he was—he loaned a pair of boots to Klint, in any event, but I have not read or heard that he ever hurt anyone.

Nor can I imagine why Pellegrina would have thought so. He cannot have caused her any suffering herself. The impossibility of that is explained or established by the author when he says that she views her new acquaintance in St. Gallen as someone whom she cannot imagine involving himself in human relationships. Indeed, the reader of your story gets the impression that Pellegrina spends a painless, perhaps a happy time in St. Gallen with the young man while he is writing his book, and that for her it must be a satisfaction—in her special circumstances, an unusual or unique experience—to develop so much confidence in him that she can tell him her story. One could easily imagine her doing this with Ahasverus himself had he revealed his identity to her, and from this, precisely because of the inequality between them, a rich relationship could have developed. But it is unfortunate that her thinking is so confused that—immediately following the information he has given her—on her own she misconstrues his identity.

And finally it is unfortunate for the author of the original story that Pellegrina says to her friend: "Perhaps I shall have to drink your blood." It is true that she has admitted to being a vampire, but she did so in special circumstances and when she was upset. She is not, in reality, a vampire and in general she would prefer to avoid drinking other people's blood. Please allow me to add that even a real, orthodox vampire would scarcely wish to drink, in particular, the blood of the Eternal Jew.

I hope I have not offended you in any way by analyzing your fascinating fantasy for myself. The above is "for next time."

This letter is different from all of the others I have from Karen Blixen. She could be decisive, angry, pedantic, consoling, and helpful, and she could be in need of company, literary commentary, or advice, but whatever her mood she would remain the same and would stay behind her unassailable borders. Here her mood is different, as if her center had been touched, and one can detect in the letter a delicate, melancholy, almost anxious tone, even in her criticism of the reviewer/author. As in her other writings, she deliberately maintains her naiveté in her discussion of the New Testament—"according to the standard interpretation"—but it is obvious that more is at stake. In fact, the letter ends with a request to me not to pursue my notions any farther, but since I had assumed in her regard the kind of obligation for which she had devised the motto: "*je responderai*," I did not obey and replied to her at once, in part as follows:

The basic idea in my little story is that there are two kinds of persons who can bear witness about fire, the one who has received it and the one who has been burnt by it. But for both the contact with the element will produce the same result: what is sluggish and heavy will be easily burned away; both will undergo a purification that will cause their blood with its weight of physical passions to become transformed into something like the sap of plants. I had in mind the Rosicrucian image of the black cross with the seven roses at the intersection of the beams. The roses "signify" that the heavy, difficult and anxious human blood has become as light and cool and obedient as flower sap. Those beings, who either willingly or unwillingly have been burned porous, can, as witnesses, without taking part in other people's lives, be disturbing things to have in the world, in that they so greatly expand the realm of the possible because they, precisely as "things", have acquired a kind of permanence, and thereby, though in a painful way, demand something of people who of course want to live and have permanence.

When the young Jew in my letter, upon reflection, says that his *"real* work has always been to inflict pain," I meant that he, somewhat to his own surprise, was putting the following two things together: I bear witness—and—what has this witness provoked in those who have received it? And then he realizes: I have troubled them, upset them, a fire from heaven has gone through me to them.

With my two sketches for short stories a new tension or uneasiness came into the relationship between us. When I next visited her she asked me whether I personally had experienced the thing I had written my sketch about, and when I had to say, "No, but I can imagine it," she fell silent. Later that day, which we spent together, she asked me: "And when are you going to begin throwing stones at me?" The question hurt me, as did her remark: "The first time I saw you walk into the green parlor, I said to myself that here was a man who could get the better of me." But I was not there to get the better of her or to throw stones at her. Since she continued to circle around the matter, I thought it best to put it behind us. I borrowed an expression she often used: "Put a flower in my hair and spare it on my coffin." With this as a model I wrote a couple of verses that, like Jacob's

in Holberg's "Erasmus Montanus," were "very poor in form
but very good in content":

> *"Throw no stones*
> *when I am dead*
> *Throw one now*
> *at my head"*
> *is your demand,*
> *one I cannot*
> *understand.*
>
> *To end our row,*
> *take, noble brow,*
> *as greeting and thanks*
> *this precious stone.*

To the note I attached a small jade stone that my wife
had allowed me to take from one of her necklaces.

## 6.

Around January of 1957 the pressure of the kundalini
force in my head had become so strong that I could hardly
stand it. I also had frequent attacks of hyperventilation that
made me feel like a freshly uncorked champagne bottle. It
was a difficult situation, for I could not go to my family doctor
and say: Doctor, there is something wrong with my kundalini. My yoga teacher, the proximate cause of my problem,
could not help me. She advised me either to visit a famous
yogi in Paris or to contact someone not so well known in
Denmark who counseled on these matters and who had a
reputation in occult circles. For many reasons I chose the
latter, and I became student of his for the next four years.
He was the leader of the very small Rosicrucian Society
of Denmark and considered yoga an antiquated path of spir-

itual research. The emphasis in the program of exercises to which he introduced me, which were drawn from Rudolf Steiner's unorthodox training books, was on self-awareness. The idea was to bring one's consciousness by progressive steps into one's body and then to move it in the opposite direction of those physical exercises that overwhelmed consciousness with alien, unexaminable material. It was a kind of self-reflection designed to proceed through one's individual subjectivity into the anonymous and general spheres with which as a body and a soul one is connected. In reality, my two sketches for short stories from the previous year anticipated the mode of thinking I was now taking up. The central exercise, around which the others were coordinated like concentric rings, consisted of visualizing conflictual experiences from one's life in reverse sequence and focusing on the figure of oneself in the series of recollected images. This peculiar technique is very effective. It allows detachment from customary modes of consciousness; sooner or later one is able to see oneself, that is, to see the conglomeration of affects with which one has been identified. But prior to that encounter, which is extraordinarily unpleasant—if for no other reason than because those tendencies one has held in check and merely tried to satisfy in imagination have left traces at least as marked as those to which one has yielded—there is a long, thoroughgoing disorganization of ordinary consciousness. One moves outside of it, and outside of it one is, temporarily, *no one.*

In writing and speaking to my new teacher, I had some of the same language problems as I had had with my yoga teacher. I came to him with the standard set of Danish concepts overlaid with a literary/academic training. However, the people I was now dealing with had lived for years in a sphere of language and experience considered by the official institutions of learning, at best, as hysterical. But since these experiences compose a series as functional and orderly as one's sense experiences, the people who have them cannot be in doubt about their reality and significance—or about the academic institution's narrowmindedness. Here one must also bear in mind that these people do not compose a unified group; they do not have a common language; and there is among them a tendency for individuals to set up shop as esoteric private teachers who, in a difficult and eclectic terminology, rewrite their private experiences into vague and nebulous systems. Much the same can be said of the books they write. They do not get reviewed; they are hardly aired in public; and even when they have been written with the author's life blood, which is often the case, the huge solitude of their origin tends to cloud the truth at their core with a stubborn shadow of the provincial and the bizarre. Under these conditions it is hard to receive instruction, particularly if one tries to use contemporary language. In an ordinary conversation the speakers know what they are talking about and can refer to it as something objective, but in these other kind the subject matter cannot be separated from the person of the teacher. As I finally had to say to my new teacher: It's as if I had apprenticed myself to Jacob Boehme and he demanded that I learn shoemaking before we could start talking about theosophy.

I would not have persevered during this difficult year, which also turned out to be my life's turning point, had I not begun to receive nightly visits from Goethe. He would appear in my dreams either in the guise of a Wagner singer—my yoga teacher had been trained as a Wagner singer—or as a bedridden patient lying in the attic of Rungstedlund. Despite Goethe's fame, I had never before been able to interest myself in him because of his boring reputation at the university as a monolith of bourgeois harmony and cool self-sufficiency. This image could not have been more in disharmony with the tendency of my own inhibited and hectic temperament to gravitate toward the schizophrenic and the modern. Soon I discovered that Goethe had known crises and dividedness as well as anyone, but that he had also known healing and the resolution of crises. Things I could not understand when my esoteric teacher presented them to me in his religious terminology I suddenly recognized and comprehended when I heard them in Goethe's artistic, humane, and humorous language.

These changes in my way of thinking led me to reconsider my relationship with Karen Blixen. Instead of trying to figure her out I began to investigate which aspects of my personality she had until now been effortlessly able to control. Among other things, I realized that our relationship had been one in which a distinguished, wise, and famous old lady was supervising the education of a less-polished young man. Even if there was some truth in this, the ceremoniousness of it masked or repressed the more important fact that our relationship was also a life and death struggle about truth and love that could not, or ought not, be regulated by considerations of politeness. And so in my subsequent visits to her I began to behave more in accord with this fundamental fact and to pay less attention to the rules of respectful behavior. This did not suit her very well, and our conversations often came to an abrupt end if I posed questions that were too straightforward. Another disturbing element entered them at this time. Whenever I would talk about some problematic aspect of our relationship, a strong, clearly outlined, white swirling light would appear around the lower half of her face. The first time I saw it was in the half dark of the green parlor one late afternoon or evening. She had asked me to tell her a little about myself, and I had begun by saying: "I am my mother's son. She filled the entire house . . ." Then I paused in surprise at the sight of the lower part of her face. "Yes, I thought so," she answered, with sufficient steadiness that I was able to pull myself together and continue. After that the light would appear even in daylight whenever I approached a critical topic. Her face would take on a strangely trembling, alien expression that was painful to see. I did not want to cause her pain, but I did finally want to get to the bottom of things. This I was not able to do. It was around this time that she told me that I could speak to her or ask her about anything. So I mentioned the white light in the face that she discusses at several places in her writings, most extensively in *The Angelic Avengers*, and asked her if she could tell me more about it. We were outside taking a walk then, and a long time passed before she answered; her answer was a question: "How is Morten doing?" Morten is my son.

There are not many letters from 1957, and the few there are show clearly that the situation had become unstable. For the most part she restricted herself to the telephone. In a short letter I reply to her reproaches for not having written to her recently, a lapse she felt I would come to regret bitterly. In another one from a few months later, I find myself making the opposite sort of explanation. I had tried to get myself invited to Rungstedlund, but had been turned down on the grounds that all I ever wanted to do was talk about myself, which was not good for me. These letters of mine were a kind of stalling, for I preferred to send overdue answers than none at all; I was tired of being scolded and controlled. Tactful or not, more than tact was at stake. My method, however, could not be carried on for long, for as time went on our conversations became so brief and abrupt that they could scarcely be called conversations. She would call up, usually late at night, speak in one unbroken stretch for two or three minutes, and then say "Good night. Sleep well," and put down the receiver before I had a chance to reply. In these monologs she would tell me things about myself that I had certainly never told to anyone and that in only one or two instances could she have known from other people. "You think," she called and said to me after a month of mutual silence, "that you are the first person to experience what you are going through during these days, but thousands before you have had the same experiences." Or: "That book about Baggesen that you used to talk so much about, it is clear that you are never going to write it, and a good thing, too, because Baggesen was a demonic person impossible to understand." On a third occasion she called me up and abruptly began to give a portrait of the Norwegian author Agnar Mykle, currently on trial for pornography, in which she was nastily successful in including my own worst features before she changed the subject and began talking about Telemachos in Eyvind Johnson's *The Shores of Ithica*. "It was a pitiful portrait of Telemachos," she said. "One hadn't the slightest reason to feel sympathy for him. The only one who really understood him was the old wet nurse of heroes, Eurykleia, but she also knew that the Spirit would come. Good night. Good night."

It was crucial for me to find out the real meaning of the experiment in which I was involved. Some time after the last telephone conversation, I was at Rungstedlund on a short visit and in passing I happened to ask her whether she remembered *Wilhelm Meister*. "In part," she said. Could she answer a question for me: how Serlo, the theater director, was able to know that the Spirit would come and play Hamlet's father. "It's time for you to go now," she replied.

Each time I received one of these telephone calls at an unpredictable hour and with an unpredictable challenge, I was thrown into a state of confusion that made it impossible for me to work for several days afterward. The situation had been confused enough without them. Now it was as if she could walk in and out of me whenever she pleased. In our fifth year together, she had intentions for me that she would not reveal with a single word. She did not like Baggesen and liked Goethe even less, the petit-maître who sat in his provincial Weimar and allowed himself to be revered. He was not free like she was, or Shakespeare, or Sophus Claussen. It was true that I wanted to be free, but not at all costs— not at the cost of my wife and children, not at the cost of my conscience, if that was what she meant. One night I dreamed that she announced in public: "Aage Henriksen's garden is now a little patch in my park," and I woke up in fright. On the other hand, these raids into my territory— weren't they part of the attempt that I was making to come to terms with my old self?

It was also during this unsettling year that I began to discern a pattern in Karen Blixen's writing that I had not seen clearly before or appreciated correctly because it could not be viewed as an aspect of the piety toward nature I had initially found there. In her tales, which are constructed with an almost inconceivable precision, there is always a deep structure that contradicts or works against the sensual beauty of the surface. There is something like a filigree net of tiny meanings, repeated sentences, associations, and condensations of thought playing beneath the action of the story, all of which tend to gather around the male protagonist. Thereby a vague premonition begins to make itself felt which under the pressure of external circumstances becomes a more distinct desire, becomes interwoven with the concepts of the period, and slowly solidifies into a decision, then finally is realized in one passionate moment similar to the initial premonition that now in a split second has exhausted itself and vanished like a dream.

I found it fascinating to find these buried meanings in her texts and follow their intricacies. At the same time I also realized that in their fabulous weave an ambushing, predatory, manipulating intelligence was at work, one that was aware of the origin of desires and provided satisfaction for them in illusions. It often does this by enacting some archaic pagan ritual as if it were a Christian feast, so that vast stretches of time become implicated in the stories. While I had earlier felt equality with her, these discoveries in her texts and her telephone calls caused the distance between us to become greater and the equality less. I became frightened. My hunch at the start had now developed into the clear and distinct perception that her life was unique and unconquerable, but at the same time her stature and solitude increased beyond all measure.

# 7.

On Sunday, February 2, 1958, there was a large party at Louisiana in honor of Thorkild Bjørnvig's fortieth birthday. At the dinner table I was placed across the table from Henriette, who still visited Karen Blixen regularly. We happened to start talking about the story "Copenhagen Season" in *Last Tales*, which had been published shortly before Christmas. I had some overly intellectual and untenable ideas about it but mainly I talked about how uncomfortable the story made me feel. My objection was that while the story was interesting and full of remarkable things, it was as if the famous layer of enamel that usually enveloped her characters had in this case been replaced by a layer of sugar icing. I knew as I was talking that in a few days my words would be reported at Rungstedlund, and that not long afterward my telephone would ring. Things went as I expected and yet entirely differently.

The following Sunday, Karen Blixen called in the afternoon. In an almost inaudible voice she said that she was very ill. If I wanted to see her again while she was still alive, I would have to come at once. Now, it was not unthinkable that she was about to die, for what was unthinkable was that she was still alive. Very upset, I hung up the telephone and left at once for her home.

She was lying in the bedroom beside the green parlor, vanishingly tiny and weak. "How are you now?" "Very bad," she answered. I sat down by her bed. In this meltingly urgent hour, all my fine dinner-table talk about a tale that really did not matter to me was wiped out, and what had always been there, a mutual feeling beyond all understanding or reason, was the only reality. After I had sat there for a while, however, she brought up *Last Tales* and asked me what I thought about "Copenhagen Season." Choosing my words carefully, I managed to tell her my real opinion, adding that it bothered me a little that Adelaide, who by and large was a sweet girl and not an outrageous or sacrilegious person, had to be struck by the most improbable misfortunes. She replied that she understood my opinion. Which story did I like best? I said I supposed the ones about Angelo.

During Christmas I had circled in bewilderment around these stories, particularly "The Cloak." In this story, a transmission of power and soul occurs from one person to another; it happens in the instant when the old master takes the cloak off his own shoulders and puts it on Angelo's. I had seen this, for I had become enormously attentive to the finest details in her stories. But at the same time, I was feeling such a bubbling of subtle energy in me that only with great difficulty could I grasp complete designs and consequences. I now began to talk about this story and to connect the night Angelo spends in prison as a hostage for his teacher, during which he is split apart at a fundamental level, with the events of the recent years between her and me. "I don't really understand what you are talking about," she said.

Then the conversation died away, and some time went by before I noticed that the space between us was like it was alive, as it had been with my yoga teacher but now in a different way. Energy was radiating from her, growing stronger and stronger until it felt like a hard, dry wind coming out of the marrow of her bones and that made my eyes water. When I raised my head and looked at her, she was almost hidden in a cloudy scarlet aura in which white swirling phosphorescent lights were rotating like a disk. God knows how I looked myself—like a friend at a deathbed or like a thief? The phenomenon lasted for a long time, though I am not sure how long, perhaps ten minutes.

She was the one to break our silent, intense contact by saying in a short, dry voice: "Come now," as if we had concluded an agreement. The situation was developing and changing from moment to moment. Once again a meeting with Karen Blixen had slowly transformed itself into an optical instrument in which the impurities of one's own heart became visible. I knew that if I went with her now I would come to a place that I knew nothing about, but even if the earth had begun to quake it would not have occurred to me that I could still break off and go away. I came over and sat on the edge of the bed and leaned down over her, as she indicated that I should, at the same time sending out my thoughts for help and protection for both of us. Then she put both of her hands around my neck and bored one finger deep and hard into the back of my neck, and ended by stroking me in a downward movement over my shoulders. When

I straightened up she broke the silence with the unexpected command: to recite a verse. The first to come into my head were the opening lines of Sarastro's aria in *The Magic Flute*, lines that, as I assumed she intended, contained my understanding of what this hour meant, or what I wanted it to mean:

> *In diesen heil'gen Hallen*
> *kennt man die Rache*
> *    nicht*
> *und ist ein Mensch*
> *    gefallen*
> *führt Liebe ihn zur Pflicht.*

> (Within these holy halls
> revenge is unknown
> and if a man has fallen
> love will lead him to
> duty.)

I was dizzy when I got up from my uncomfortable position. It was as if the entire lower part of my body had drawn together in a cramp and was sending strong streams up into my head. I wanted to say something, but she stopped me: "Go now."

As I write down for the first time the events of that afternoon twenty-five years ago, they are as clear to me as if they had happened yesterday. She died many years ago, and soon I will be as old as she was when I met her.

When I woke up the following morning, it was as if I had a lump of lead in my neck. During the following days the blockage increased and became more painful. I had frequent attacks of migraine with feelings of nausea and dizziness. At the same time the block closed off the stream of kundalini energy to my head, with the result that my head began to shake. One evening, when I was getting ready and was standing in front of the bathroom mirror, I saw a bright red glow about an inch above both of my shoulders. For a long time I did not know whether I was saved or lost. To involve other people in the matter seemed for the time being impossible, since there were so many aspects of it that I could not present to any doctor. Some years later, when my condition had become somewhat stable, the thought occurred to me that perhaps I had a prolapsed disk in my neck, and I visited many kinds of therapists. For two periods of time I went to a physiotherapist; I have been put in traction at the National Hospital; I have seen a chiropractor, tried Mensendieck exercises, and received curative massage, each time with the same result: the treatment made the pains worse. Only after a couple of months would they subside back to their usual level. The first five to six years were the worst; after that the pains stayed within the limits of the tolerable. Most of the time I can keep my head still. Its shaking used to be very embarrassing and created awkward situations. People who were a little unsure of themselves tended to think that I was constantly shaking my head in disapproval of them, which did not improve the impression people had of me.

From my letters I can see that I visited her in March and April and continued to act as her literary consultant. Otherwise I do not remember much of what we said to each other, except that neither of us ever mentioned that afternoon when, instead of dying, she revealed herself to be incomprehensibly full of life. One occasion, however, that I do remember very clearly was "a young people's party" she held one afternoon in the late spring. It must have been in May, for the sun was shining and the weather was so warm that we could walk around outside without overcoats. Elsa Gress, Bent Mohn, and Juri Moskovitn were there, among numerous others. My head was shaking like an old mandarin's, I was full of doubt and very tense, and later I got the impression that I did not make many friends for myself that day. It was not a successful party, which was not Karen Blixen's fault, other than that the weight of her personality in the opinion of her guests precluded an unconstrained and easy conversation. She tried to improve the mood by with-drawing for a while, but it did not work, at least not with me. It would have been better for us to see the situation for what it was and sit down in a circle around her.

At a certain moment, the party took a leisurely stroll up to Ewald's Hill and back down again. On the way up, Karen Blixen came over to me and arranged it so that we were walking behind the others. She pointed out to me that I had not made use of the generous offer she had made me some months ago, to come up to Rungstedlund whenever I wanted without first having to telephone. She was at my disposal; I could call her at night if there was anything I wanted to talk to her about. I had nothing to reply, for what she said was true enough.

On the way back down, we found the rest of the party waiting by the bridge beside the little lake. They wanted to feed the ducks but needed someone to fetch some food. "You are going to do it, Dr. Henriksen," she said in a loud voice. "And you are going to run down to Mrs. Carlsen and back again as fast as you possibly can."

What sort of a demonstration was that? What was she thinking of? That I had so cut myself off from all of my other friends and so attached myself to her that now, like some sort of faint-hearted nincompoop, all I could do was recite: "Roses are red/ Violets are blue/ Whatever Karen Blixen says/ That's what I do"?

"I will be happy to fetch the duck food," I answered, "but at my own pace."

"Well then there is no point in doing it," she replied. Someone did get the duck food, and quickly, but it was some-one who was able to run faster than I.


## 8.

In the apprenticeship I had just completed, Karen Blixen had been my fixed point of reference. Her thin figure had been the trunk around which I had wound myself like a vine and learned from; from her power over me I had tried to free myself, and had learned from the attempt; and by the genius of her writings my eyes had been opened to paths and transformations of consciousness that I would never have discovered on my own. Whenever I had left her to go my own way, I had met her sitting at the next crossroads, waiting for me. I had learned more from her than from all of the schools I had ever attended. All thought of breaking with her and writing off our years together as a misunderstanding was unthinkable. And yet to continue our relationship now, when every meeting with her exposed me to unpredictable reversals and attacks, was not possible either. In the following years our connection grew very thin, and for a long time I refused to visit her when she would call and ask me to come. Once again I needed to put some order in my thoughts. I did so, and in the process found that doors to chambers of thought that had been locked for me earlier began to open.

The things I had learned bore fruit in the odd four-handed music played by my Rosicruican teacher and Goethe inside me. I found in the Wilhelm Meister novels the experiences and borderline struggles that I had been living with for years; the same was true of the magical fruits of my yoga year, but now in novel form and not as short stories, and it was the coherence of the novel I needed now. Crises, reversals, self-deceptions—these were all there, but not as inalterable pentagrams or ultimate defeats. Misfortunes loomed up, caused suffering and despair, then subsided and provoked reflection. Reflection found new openings for itself at the same time as new opportunities appeared in the world, as if these two had long been waiting for each other. Goethe offered me all of this, and the meeting with him brought me incomparable liberation and relief. Even my most painful memories became washed along in that broad epic stream and showed themselves as foolish but not as fatal. By spiritually letting myself be lifted up a little by him, I was able at the same time to come back down to earth, and late but sweet came the neglected joys of youth to us.

I began to see that the universe into which Karen Blixen had introduced me was populated by people who in one significant regard shared the same conception: that it is not the experience of objects but the state of one's consciousness that is the human being's most immediate experience, even if it takes a long time before one is able to observe it, which means that the contradictions derived by thought from sense experience veil the true nature of consciousness. Thus people experience themselves on one level and make decisions and act on another, an existential imbalance that can be resolved pedagogically or exploited seductively, depending on how the more insightful self is disposed and positioned in life. Both parts are equally aware that a person's true identity is not the mask he must wear in social circumstances, where he is subject to the concepts of a superficial moral purity, but his hidden face, with all of the scars his passions, fantasies, and disappointments have inflicted on it. Karen Blixen had written to me about this some years previously, in a way that at the time I could not understand. I was trying to write an essay with the tentative title "Karen Blixen and Masks" and was using "The Deluge at Norderney" as a point of departure. It seemed to me that the small party of people in the hayloft at Norderney was more like a number of playing cards than people, and I thought I saw a kind of geometric symmetry in the way they were arranged: Kasparson, who aspires to be revered as a saint at any price, versus the chaste Miss Nat-og-Dag, who has used up her erotic resources in perverse imaginary debauches. I indicated a little of what I was thinking to Karen Blixen, and she replied:

I wonder whether you will be able to understand this or find it useful: It is quite true she is positioned "symmetrically" opposite Kasparson, in the sense that K., who is corrupt, achieves final fulfillment in the saint's role, while she, as a kind of eternal innocence—because of the nature of the world (among other things, the Pietists' preconceived notion of its corruption) and as if playing a game in all seriousness, since that is the kind of game she plays best, has had to find her fulfillment by impersonating the great whore. When Kasparson at last proudly confesses his guilt, she confesses—"I want to tell you something too—my entire life"—with a kind of proud modesty (because after all the world is as it is), her eternal innocence or *tabula rasa* quality, her forest goddess nature. The author's (astoundingly) optimistic view of life reveals itself here in that the two of them meet in mutual confidence and harmony, "in light", in something that for these two, in terms of the logic of the story, must be taken as salvation—also because she, even if she has had to wait for, and now at last happily accept, his slogan: to laugh back etc., is in reality superior to him. Does this make sense to you?

When I received this letter in 1954 it did not make much sense to me, and I gave up my idea of writing an essay, but in the years between 1958 and 1960 it did prove useful. In those years I finally put together my book on Baggesen. And I dare say that even if that memorable afternoon at her bedside did not go exactly as she had planned, since my head, though wobbly, remained in place and eventually grew fast again, it nevertheless changed me. It was not as in *Hadding's Saga*, where the old woman twists the head off a cock and throws it over the wall, whereupon it starts to crow on the other side. On the other hand, my voice did change and I began to see connections I had never seen before. In my book *The Traveler* I was able to make good use of the experiences of my apprentice years, for the years around 1800 were years of high spiritual tension in which Kant's philosophy, occult currents, powerful and distinguished noblewomen, and revolutionary political movements fought for sovereignty over people's consciousness. I could use the tension, which from a historical standpoint was incomprehensible, between Goethe and Karen Blixen as a secret inner principle of composition, just as I could also use the even more fortunate circumstance that at that time Goethe was the one who was physically present, and she absent.

After the long moonlit night, the true light of day was

beginning to dawn. But—it was as if she had a part in that, too, and as if it were *that* which I had wanted from her most of all. Was not the rising sun beginning to shine on me through the figure of a woman? She had told me that when her mother died she had kept watch by the body through the night, and that then she had understood the long logic in a mother's life that is otherwise hidden to a daughter. And she had told me it would be the same for me when she died. In my literary way I was keeping watch over a dead woman who was still alive and rediscovering her youth. That was why on the title page of my book I placed an old picture of a woman standing on a sickle moon with the light of the sun shining through her.

A few weeks before *The Traveler* was due to be published, some time in April of 1961, she called up and said that now she definitely thought I ought to come and visit her. "Now I would like to," I answered, and the following day I was there.

She had, by the time I arrived, unquestionably read my book in galley form, but she did not mention it. Wasting no time, she went directly to what was on her mind, and that day I was sufficiently composed to be able to say what was on mine, more or less, in the way that I wanted to say it. I reproduce the conversation in a slightly abridged form, because I cannot remember all of it; for example, I cannot remember exactly how she managed to place the surprising remark that I had been one of her lovers, a remark that in her mouth did not mean what it usually means and which I could only answer with a questioning look.

"I would like you to tell me what you think of me," she said.

"I do know one thing, that you are more than I am."

"Yes, that is true. But do you also think that I am an honest and upright person?"

"That . . . um. Tell me one thing. What really happened between us that Sunday afternoon more than three years ago, when you pressed your finger into the back of my neck?"

"What you are saying now has never happened. It must be something you dreamed."

"I see. But then honesty is something I have never demanded or expected from you. When I say to you that you are more than I am, I also mean that I cannot judge whether honesty, in the ordinary sense of the term, is possible between us. You have done many things to me that I could not have allowed myself to do to another person, if I had been able to. And I don't know whether you had a right to do them either; the only thing I will say is that the greatest happiness in my life has been that I met you.

"In the first years after you pressed your finger into my neck, I didn't know whether I was going to live or die, and I still have strong pains there, but I've never for a second been able to feel bitter toward you. The pains are there, but on the other hand my depression is gone, and it was worse. Now, however, I have reached a limit I dare not cross. I can't take any more."

"I see that we won't be seeing each other any more."

"No, we won't. You've told me many times that I am going to have many things to regret in your regard. But I don't think so. I've always done my utmost with you, also when I have been stupid or vain, and if in the future I come to understand things better, I will have to console myself with the thought that I did what I could.

"It seems to me that you have opened two paths for me. As far as I can understand, you are pointing very definitely in the one direction; but the fact that the other one, the one I want to take, has become visible to me, is also something that I owe to you."

She gestured to me that I should kiss her, but I had decided in advance that I would not let myself be overwhelmed by any sentimentality that might be brought into the situation. Nor did I dare, and I told her that I did not want to. "Well go then, you strange and stingy person, and find happiness on the way you have chosen."

A few weeks later, I sent her my book with the following

dedication: "Out of the eater came something to eat. Out of the strong came something sweet," which is Samson's riddle in the Book of Judges. She replied with a quotation from the same book, and these are Karen Blixen's final words to me: "Thank you. Now tell me, my dear, I pray thee, wherewith thou mightest be bound."

C H A P T E R   6

# The Empty Space Between Art and Church

## Translated by Annette Wernblad

If it is true, as so many women claim today, that women make up not only half of the population but also half of the meanings of life, then it is true today only because it has always been so. But then the assertion opens up the prospect of historical critique and elucidation that have to do not only with various forms of cohabitation but with morality and theology as well.

When Karen Blixen as one of her standard paradoxes professed that she was three thousand years old, then probably it is a linguistic short form that was meant to indicate the historical span of her consciousness of the constant but often unseen presence of the feminine. The formula for this presence she herself has outlined in *Daguerreotypes*: "It is the secret power of the feminine: the intimated." The meaning of this sentence is not that women distinguish themselves by special intuitions but that they arouse notions in the male consciousness with their faces and bodies and—when they become aware of this—by signs and words and actions. Thereby they participate, even when they seem not to participate, and when they do not control the steps of men, they

177

control their thoughts. Thus the erotic sphere has a far wider extension than one would ordinarily assume, and it turns out to be a consciousness-shaping force. I am quite aware that this is not satisfactory as a feminist basis today, where everything is a question of social visibility, but this point of view opens up the prospect for other perspectives that would have otherwise been closed. As a matter of fact, this rests on our childhood knowledge that a human being is a man and a woman, as it says in Genesis, and this admits us to areas where we thought mankind was not allowed.

With these introductory remarks I have opened up a vast and airy space. I shall now attempt to build a staircase ascending it.

In one of her shortest tales, "The Fish," Karen Blixen has delineated the prototype that is the basis of all of her stories. It concerns a young nineteen-year-old girl. A week ago she was married to the young squire of whom she has been fond since they played together as children. They have had some trouble marrying each other, but now things are settled and she enthusiastically takes command over her little kingdom. It is—quite as she has been told that reality is—a small, orderly, and decent place that is suspended in a larger, overall lawfulness and decency. She has found her place. Her dreams of reality coincide with what she sees around her—and she imagines an endless line of carefree, happy days. Now she can fully expose her inner being and nothing hidden or secret can come between her husband and herself. But a week after her wedding, in a clearing in the woods, she is accidentally confronted with a hunted outlaw, a boy her own age. His face is bruised and smashed, his hands are dark and soiled, and his clothes are torn to shreds. This sight upsets her and she is frightened, not of what he might do to her but by the fact that he exists, for he is incompatible with her idea of reality. But within the few moments they face each other, he begins to exist for her. At the moment when he attempts to, as it were, extinguish himself by closing his eyes and setting her free, he becomes real for her. And when she is back in the open park once more, safe and unharmed, she feels that she has devoted herself to something. "To what? To poverty, outlawry, total desolation. To the sin and sorrow of the entire world." Concealing her newfound insight, she rejoins her husband—with the insurmountable secret like a wall between them.

In miniature, this recognition is the underlying principle of all of Karen Blixen's works. Parallels can be drawn to the Book of Job, the biblical text that Blixen quotes most often and most convincingly. Honest-to-the-core Job too, as you know, falls silent when he sees his orderly and simple reality transformed into a dream, which is let into a larger, more dangerous, unpredictable reality that includes everything which criminally and sacredly lies outside the law.

The process of thought that is indicated here is not, of course, entirely surprising. It has been at work in the European consciousness during the last 150 years. For Marx and Freud and the natural sciences, visible everyday life, regulated by good sense and morality, is merely a reflection of impersonal forces that never even reach the consciousness of those who act in an everyday world. Unlike these predominant modes of thought, however, Karen Blixen does not arrive at her ideas of the subconscious via theoretical constructions or laboratory experiments. Like so many of the great women writers of our time, among them Iris Murdoch and Doris Lessing, Blixen is at one and the same time a storyteller and a thinker. This double focus of the consciousness means that she always has to start within the everyday lives of the people who wish, act, and speak. Her subject could, with Goethe's expression, be called the "apparent secrets," the secrets that are just in front of one's eyes but which only a few experience and reflect on. In that way, with her completely attentive observation and empathetic imagination for consequences, slowly she created a universe for herself, which simultaneously was modern, highly original, and ancient.

There is not much doubt of how she first arrived at these ideas. The shape in which she first encountered the subconscious and the invisible was the traditionally religious one.

As is well known, she grew up in an environment where discourse was governed by a strictly moralistic Christianity. This became an indelible part of her own consciousness as well, although she turned against it in opposition. What she heard did not correspond with what she saw. Out of this conflict grew a desire to recapture the visible, sensual, natural world and to pursue the natural passions to their farthest, most hidden recesses.

Several years after she had made her first decisions in this matter, she displayed them as part of a speech she gave for Ole Wivel on her sixty-fifth birthday. The most obvious occasion was that Ole Wivel and Martin A. Hansen, as the new editors of the literary periodical *Heretica*, had announced a new direction that would merge art with moral responsibility. This brought her to speak on the ambiguous and sensuous nature of art that undermines any moralization and about the conflict between a religious and a heroic-atheistic view of life that she knew from childhood and that—in Africa—was a perfectly resolved and reconciled conflict. Heavenly love and earthly love were not regarded as contradictions out there as they are with the Christian Europeans, as apparently they were in Martin A. Hansen and now in *Heretica*: a contagion from the dualistic tradition itself. "I am warning you," she continued, "against your moral choice and inclinations towards the ethical. Has not this exact choice in our protestant cultures led us, against our very own intentions, straight into the abyss? Has not Christianity excluded the enthusiasm over the gifts and mysteries of this life, renounced and repressed our sensuality? And thereby blocked us out of the spiritual world on the only conditions that we have." Later in her speech she mentioned that in her youth she had heard two of the outstanding personalities of the Danish folk high school movement, Holger Begtrup and Jakob Knudsen, give public speeches and had felt repelled. Only later did she realize that the reason for her reaction was that these two men, who were powerful and articulate, and more than slightly conceited, spoke against their own charisma—about the fragility and impotence of the human race.

Her observation is of the kind that we know so well from many literary works, which austerely reveal how the things men say and imagine are meant merely to obscure the much feebler things they do and are. But Karen Blixen makes a different use of the well-known instrument than the conventional. She uses it not as a moral tool for castigation but, on the contrary, to show how the natural passions deeply pervade the official virtue and unencumberedly reach their goals precisely because of the slack and vague character of virtue and piety.

This attitude, now, has two far-reaching consequences, both of which are surprising, and while I develop the first, the second cannot be inferred. The first is that a certain pattern, one could call it a genre within the narrative genre, is repeated in Blixen's works. A ceremony takes place. It is conducted like a familiar Christian feast or festival, the Sacrament or celebration of Pentecost, but if one takes a closer look, it turns out that what is really conducted under this pious cover is a pagan mystery. The major example of this is "The Deluge at Norderney"; in a more compact form it is repeated in "The Heroine," "Babette's Feast," and "The Last Day." I shall have to limit myself to discussing the shorter texts.

The stories are based on the undeniably well-known fact about human love relationships, that they are complicated. As in the animal world, one sex is attracted to the other, but if that were the whole matter, then already at this point love would be as uncomplicated as Lenin assumed it would be after the revolution: "As simple as drinking a glass of water." But, as we all know, this general instinct is most powerfully unleashed in the meeting of two individuals. *People* fall in love. Their individuality, their social identities, are pervaded by the nature of their instincts, and from this circumstance emanate all of the well-known deformations, illusions, and breakthroughs to surprising discoveries that love is probably not what at first we thought it was.

The horizontal solution to the problems of love is so familiar, so excellent that it is unnecessary for me to mention or recommend it. On the other solution, however, I shall have to dwell for a few moments. We could call it the vertical solution, because up and down pervade each other, the instinctual impulses rise and pour themselves into consciousness and self-consciousness.

What we are talking about here, of course, is the individualization of the impulses. You could argue that all magic tricks and artifices on erotic grounds, in fiction, in psychoanalysis, and in day-to-day reality, consist of interfering with and fracturing the psychosomatic system, in which the anonymous and the individual desires are united. An object picture might be useful here. In Jakob Burchardt's *The Renaissance in Italy* is printed a reproduction of a picture by the painter Angelo Bronzino, entitled *Lucrezia*. It portrays a beautiful woman who is staring searchingly, straight out of the picture at the spectator. Her right breast is exposed and swelling out at the observer, who might feel attracted were it not for the fact that in her left hand, extended upward, she is holding a long pointed knife, which one must assume to be as sharp as it is pointed.

Simultaneously she urges, allures, and repels, but what in this manner is elicited and incapable of reaching its object subsequently goes its own inner ways. This Lucrezia, with her ambiguous appearance, calls to mind the biblical Judith, whose story is told in one of the Apocrypha. When I mention her here it is because soon we shall reencounter her. She defeats Holofernes, Israel's enemy, by means of her beauty alone: "She anointed her face with ointment and fastened her hair with a tiara and put on a linen gown to deceive him. Her sandal ravished his eyes, her beauty captivated his mind, and the sword severed his neck."

This might be the right time to remind you that this ambiguity of the erotic, which I have suggested, has played a crucial part up through European history in Christian sects and lodges. There an attempt was made to separate what is naturally united. On the one hand an ascending spiritual development was encouraged with several means, but at the same time—in the midst of societies that were narrow-minded and terrified of sex—an attempt was made to develop a liberated but controlled sensuality. The latter was not simply in an attempt to create an increased joie de vivre but also to tie up sensuality to wordly conditions, the only place where sensuality is requited. The purpose of this was to prevent sensuality from serpentinely following the spiritual stream inward and upward. In Mozart's *The Magic Flute*, this division is performed and the double wedding illustrated in a famous and festive line of images.

But in Karen Blixen's tales, it is the opposite strategy, that of merging, that governs their progress.

Most admirably and with the complete enthusiastic endorsement of the reader, this happens in the tale "The Heroine." It is set during the Franco-Prussian War in 1870 and concerns a French company of travelers who are stranded in an inn behind German lines. Their lives now depend on the young German officer who is in command there. It now turns out, to his horror and enthrallment, that the person he is to negotiate with is the dazzling French beauty Heloise. A power struggle takes place between them, which evolves so that the desires she arouses with her splendor she expels by means of unlimited impertinence and scorn. This does not exterminate his desires, which instead travel other, invisible roads within him. And it is then characteristic of Heloise, as of Blixen's other female characters and indeed of Karen Blixen herself, that, despite everything, she is capable of meeting and capturing the desires that stream toward goals that are hidden to the world, so that later she can praise their strength.

A little while ago I said that the reader enthusiastically is on Heloise's side and stands behind her, but maybe, after all, the reader of this story, whether male or female, gets a little ill at ease when the backcloths of the story are pulled up one by one. Closest behind the story one finds Maupassant's tale "Boule de suif," on which "The Heroine" clearly is paralleled. It takes place in exactly the same setting but concerns the humiliations of a woman. Behind this story emerges Rousseau's *La nouvelle Héloïse*, and behind this story about psychological destruction of love emerges the medieval romance of Heloise and Abelard and his mutilation. All the way at the back lies the myth of Venus and Adonis. And on all of these backcloths what we call love has left its traces of humiliation and violence, castration, and death.

More peculiar than the Heloise figure and surrounded with a sweeter and more beautiful magic is the fifteen-year-old girl in the tale "The Last Day." This story takes place on Whitsunday of 1852, and the opening of the tale is preoccupied with considerations over where and in what shape the Holy Spirit would emerge if on its feast day it visited Copenhagen. It does not arrive; instead Odin appears, but in the shape of one of his most alluring valkyries. *She* is described thus by the young man who first sets eyes on her in a clearing in the woods, where she emerges in a gleam:

> She was so exquisite that she beamed. She looked straight at me with her eyes wide open, like the bright eyes of a hawk, and her gaze was not mild, no, it was stern, wild, one might think that she was angry with one. But at the same time it was infinitely friendly and encouraging. She knew everything and laughed at the danger.

But I must limit myself to discussing the central scene of this complicated story, which illuminates all the others. As the adopted daughter of a minister, the above-mentioned girl takes care of an old sailor in the parish, the narrator's Uncle Valdemar. In his prime, Uncle Valdemar was a great womanizer and has many proud conquests behind him. But now, for several years, he has been sitting in his chair, paralyzed from the waist down, feeling that neither life nor death wants anything to do with him. He fears dying in the straw—just like the mythical Nordic warriors, because this would lead them down to Hel. But Uncle Valdemar's discouragement during his long and weary process of disintegration changes to hope when the minister's daughter starts to visit him. And all his hopes are redeemed on his last day, which passes thus: The girl sits and reads to him from the Bible, from the last chapter of the book of Judith, Judith's triumphal song. The old man persuades her to move closer to him, and finally he rises up by clinging to her. Also his manhood rises one last time. He kisses her while she holds on to his long white hair and his face starts to glow. "But the next moment she pushed him away with a swift, frantic movement, and thereby he tumbled down sidelong to her feet." There on the floor, now, lies Uncle Valdemar with a solemn, triumphant, glowing face. And he dies. And the young girl has the same serious, triumphantly glowing face.

She *does* break his neck, there is no denying that. But she does it out of sheer kindness, in quiet empathy, of pure technical necessity—so as to prevent the stream that has finally reached the halls of Valhalla in his skull from being sucked down again.

Excepting the final acts of Goethe's *Faust* and *The Tibetan Book of the Dead*, nowhere in literature have I encountered such intimacy with death and the arterial roads through which the soul can move.

When Karen Blixen conceived of her plan of turning against Christian morality and duality to follow the natural passions into their inner recesses instead, she was enabled to uncover experiences as ancient and forgotten as the Dead Sea Scrolls. This was the first consequence of the plan. The reader who adjusts himself to see her perspective and is perhaps even radiated by her perspicacity may identify with the young wife in "The Fish": "The world is different, unfamiliar, yet recognizable; I have to reconsider all things." Thereby we are led into the other surprising consequence of the original plan. It has to do with the costs and once again poses the problem of dualism.

What Blixen said about dualism to Ole Wivel she once wrote to me: "You say that nature has no memory, but I have often wished that I had the memory of a tree, which carries each and every single annual ring stamped into its being. I am altogether incapable of comprehending a 'dualism.' " And it *is* true: the universe of her tales is natural, erotic, and no ways out of it are indicated. But it is not so hermetic that there are no ways in—from an unknown, undescribed space of possibilities. The men who force their way into full visible identity in her tales pay for their victory with their lives. What kind of lives? The deaths they experience could be described as murders, as when the butler Kasparson kills his master, the cardinal. More often, however, these deaths are suggested merely as an imperceptible dwindling of longing, a discontinuation of the ability to love. A source of light withdraws from their lives to return to its own space.

The uneasiness that arises for the reader from these vague but perpetually repeated clues indeed harmonizes perfectly with the fact that Karen Blixen did not present herself as a person who was liberated on all sides in the terms of modern science. Quite the reverse: when I met her, and when other people met her, she said that she had died many years ago, and in the most hair-raising fashion and to the confusion and despair of her friends, she defined herself within the Christian tradition as a witch, and a serpent, and the friend of the Devil. This was not a whim, not a joke once uttered, but something that she claimed as her right, the essential note on all texts. But thus, of course, dualism reemerges in a new shape as a relationship between the life which is included in her works and that which is excluded. The tremendous expansion contains its own disintegration.

The best answer to this enigma is probably another question: Why do we, who were young thirty years ago, need precisely her and not more God-fearing individuals? Why do so many people need her today? To this question she once gave me an answer that applies to others besides myself. She said:

> As long as I live it will be bothersome for you to have to deal with me. But when I am dead, what happened to me when my mother died and I kept vigil over her at night, will happen to you. Then I saw not just the old woman,

but also the young wife, and the happy little girl. And then I understood many things I had not understood before.

This advice builds a bridge over the terrifying ambiguity in Karen Blixen's being and works, and if followed, it can lead one beyond the limits of the universe that she controlled so powerfully. Only then does what she said of herself turn out to be true: "I am a messenger who has been sent on a long journey to declare that there is hope in the world."

# CHAPTER 7

# Afterword to the American Edition

Thirty-five years separate the first from the last article in this book, so the picture they present of Karen Blixen and her writings is not entirely consistent. The first article, "Karen Blixen and Marionettes," was written before I knew her personally. It led in turn to our acquaintance, which lasted for ten years. Perhaps one would think that as I got to know her, my impression of her specialness would diminish, for obviously she, like everyone, also had an everyday life. The opposite, however, occurred. Her stature increased for me to an alarming degree and I came to see her writings in a new light. It became clear to me that here, in the frailest, the lightest of bodies, a unique condensation of psychic force had taken place, and that her life, in each of its segments, was unconquerable.

It has not been my objective to draw a harmonious picture of Karen Blixen, although some distinguished literary people think I should have done so. I heartily disagree. Such an objective consists, in the final analysis, of translating the unknown into the known and making it acceptable within the standards of conventional morality. It would be, in other words, an act of repressive tolerance, a way of killing off protest. Goethe, a generally amiable person, once broke out in anger when he found himself being discussed in terms far too benign: "You praise me, Fool, which means you think you understand me." This kind of anger is beneficial, for is is fueled by the salutary thought that things that are both high and deep ought to be allowed to persist in their strangeness, and that the possibility must always be kept open to rise above and step to one side of the culture of the average everyday.

For me, twenty-five years of reflection have not exhausted all of the secrets in Karen Blixen's writings or extinguished the magical aura around her person. This will have to suffice.

## 1.

In the twenty-five years since her death Karen Blixen has become world famous. The basis for her reputation was laid when Frans Lasson's edition of her *Letters From Africa* was translated into English, and then followed by Judith Thurman's great biography. But it was not until 1986, in the midst of the age of computers, satellites, and international terror, that the film *Out of Africa* caused the sophisticated world of the media to take her to itself as one of this century's great female myths. Which is what she had always wanted, despite the inevitable comprises involved. Only when she could see herself as a part of the frieze of internationally known faces did she have the feeling of truly existing.

This may seem surprising, for she did not pursue international celebrity in a straightforward way. Generally such fame is accorded to a superior talent when it performs in a manner immediately comprehensible to the public. Karen Blixen did not write like that. It is true that her genius in visible on the surface of her texts as style, but it is a style tightly linked to a central core and controlled with an unflagging diligence and an almost pedantic concern for detail. Her tales are so ingenious and many-leveled, so suffused with cultural tradition, so carefully brought by craft and thought to their points of soundlessly hovering suspension that they, like Nietzsche's works, have quite naturally become writings for other writers and for the most enterprising of critics. They do not address themselves to the general public. This is a fact that again became evident at the international Blixen conference which was held in 1985 at the University of Minnesota. And it *was* international; literary researchers came from many countries, though the press, even locally, paid little attention to the meeting. The composition of the meeting explains why. Among the sixty participants were no black people, and, as is usual at literary events these days, there were three or four women for every man. Among the many women (university teachers, critics, librarians) were many who were penetrating, intelligent, highly educated, versed in depth psychology and women's studies, but their voices aroused no echo outside of the conference halls. This would not have surprised Karen Blixen, who never expected much from academe, though she took from it whatever happened to come her way.

Once, when an American oil magnate paid her a polite visit at Rungstedlund, she was capable of saying afterward that it was lovely to meet people of her own kind. And when Hemingway, after he had been offered the Nobel Prize instead of her, publicly declared that she ought to have had it, she burst out: "To such heights must I be lifted in order to be seen as I really am." Such remarks could be depressing for the people around her, for they were spoken to create a distance between her and them, but they could also be confusing, for no matter how good a writer one may consider Hemingway, to speak of him in terms of "heights" is hardly appropriate.

In the story "Echoes," the young boy, Emanuele, who for several weeks has been singing with Pellegrina's former voice, says to her as he looks around her room: "I think that here I have heard my own voice coming to me from some-where else, I know not from where. I think the whole world was singing in it."* This seems to me an understandable remark, for around Karen Blixen, as around no other writer in this century, both as she was and as she became, whether she was speaking with her first or her second voice, endless and heretofore silent stretches of historical time were called into play. But the "whole world" and the fashionable world —they are not composed of the same ingredients and they are not coterminous.

She knew this, of course. One cannot take the easy way around her by pointing out her contradictions. Precisely the fact that Emanuele is singing with Pellegrina's former voice manifests the contradiction.

Nor does this mean that feelings of self-doubt prompted her demand to be considered as special or superior, as not really being present in any situation unworthy of her inter-national reputation. Rather, she emphasized her specialness at the slightest opportunity. One finally had to recognize that she did really feel this way about herself and that this feeling formed the basis for some of her less estimable friendships—it was a side of her personality one could not ignore. This attitude of hers is perhaps best illustrated by the last example I shall mention, which perhaps shows her in a less than flattering light.

She was once telling me about Negley Farson's appear-ance in Copenhagen's Student Union one evening in the 1930s. Famous at the time, the American journalist, traveler, and adventurer had been invited to hold a speech about his new book, *The Way of a Trangressor.* Karen Blixen was among the invited guests. The evening did not go as planned, how-ever, for the speaker, on reaching the podium, turned out to be dead drunk. "And," said Karen Blixen, "in the front

---

*The last sentence of this quotation appears only in the Danish version of the story.—TRANS.

row sat all the little Danish professors swelling up with indignation, while for my part I wanted to go up and give him
a big hug."

The anecdote perhaps contains a clue, for we know what
she thinks about professors. They are people with a great
amount of knowledge about a certain subject and alongside
of it a private life totally unrelated to the subject. But those
others, those in whose ranks Karen Blixen wished to be
counted, have no private life, for they have thrown it into
their endeavors. Their exploits and their destiny have become one, and they have taken on the simplicity of
emblems—Hemingway, Marilyn Monroe, Muhammad Ali.
"No one has had such a bloody entrance to literature as I,"
Karen Blixen once said in an interview, after having been
identified as the author of *Seven Gothic Tales*.

Here is something—despite all of the obvious
differences—reminiscent of identity in the religious sense.
All of the reserves of the person have been used up and
translated into visibility. Insights have been achieved that
cannot be spoken, or if spoken they are not heard, not grasped.

In John Fowles's novel *The Magus*, the old man says
one day to his student, the object of his experiment, "Come.
I am now going to show you life's innermost secret." He
takes and places him in front of an ancient sculpture of a
face bearing a smile of triumph, and he says: "This is truth.
Not hammer and sickle. Not stars and stripes. Not the cross.
Not the sun. Not gold. Not Yin and Yang. But the smile. . .
This is truth. Truth is irreconcilable."

The smile confronting the young man is not the floating,
enlightened, introverted smile of the Buddha but the smile
of someone who has gone through everything, gone through
the unthinkable, and has not been conquered. It could as
well have been the face of Karen Blixen.

## 2.

It is said that great personal strength comes from the resolution of internal contradictions. Doubtless this is true. But the reflexive path back to the energies inhibited by the difficulties of birth and maturation was not the one Karen Blixen chose. She went resolutely and unconquerably forward, so that in the balance sheet of her fame are a touching number of painful, irreversible losses—the early loss of her father, of her health, of her lover, of her farm, of subsequent friends. The contradictions she met on her way she absorbed in a different way: she made use of them, she lodged herself in them and kept their tension alive in herself. The identifying characteristic of the central poetic figures in her tales is that they have appropriated all of the culture's religious and moral values, which they then use as a mask. With this mask as a means of social accommodation and external legitimation, they unleash a power that comes from a completely different source: the ancient, wild creative power that is utterly unconcerned with human order and morality.

Does this risky game lead to a life that is more real, truer, and more valid than the ones other people live, with their anxiety and their outworn beliefs? No. Karen Blixen, with her constantly startling artistic honesty, never wrote that it did. Rather, it leads to impressive, spectacular lives constantly undermined by the awareness of being cut off from life's innermost centerpoint and meaning. In this scrupulously maintained ambiguity lies Blixen's honor and greatness. One wonders at times, when one considers the countless numbers of her admirers around the world, whether they have been able to see the careful notation of the costs incurred that Blixen has woven into the brilliant exploits in her tales. Or if instead one must have ventured very far into her universe before her account book becomes legible.

When Kasparson, the pseudocardinal who is the central character in "The Deluge at Norderney," tells the story of Barabbas, he transposes a sense of the meaning and direction of things into a sphere beyond his grasp and that was destroyed, as far as he was concerned, the moment he killed the real cardinal.

And in "The Dreamers," which is Karen Blixen's first great fictionalization of her life and her lovers, one finds running like a stream beneath the colorful images and episodes a sense, affirmed in the title, that these lives are lacking in real human substance.

The theme receives its first full exposition when Mira Jama, the narrator, is telling Lincoln about the dreams he has at night. " 'I do not know about it, Mira; I hardly ever dream,' said Lincoln." Whereupon Mira Jama breaks out, delighted at Lincoln's innocence, as one who is well aware of the difference between reality and dream:

> Oh, Lincoln, live forever. . . You dream indeed more than I do myself. Do I not know dreamers when I meet them? You dream awake and walking about. You will do nothing yourself to choose your own ways: you let the world form itself around you, and then you open your eyes to see where you will find yourself. This journey of yours, tonight, is a dream of yours. (P. 277)

To choose one's own way means to hold to a course that has been set by one's self, and that, running between internal and external impulses, takes from them the material with which to create one's true identity.

At least Lincoln is a good learner, for later, when he is recounting his first meeting with Pellegrina, he uses the same words about her that Mira Jama used about him. He says that "she was so full of life and so full of power" that it was beyond his comprehension how a woman could be like that. He later finds that his first impression of enormous strength was not entirely accurate. When he was a boy he had been trained in all circumstances to sail against the wind, while she, on the other hand, was like a ship that needed to go with the tide and a strong favoring wind. For such a ship to give itself the honor for its swiftness would not really be right, but neither would it really be wrong if, among all ships, it was the only one to know how to ally itself with the elements and enroll them in her service. "And still, at that time I did not know at all to what extent she had allied herself with all the winds and currents of life."

It is remarkable to see this image of the ship recurring twenty-five years later, when she is attempting the last great synthesis of her life and is underway into her last transformation. It happens in *Shadows on the Grass*. At that point Africa was long behind her, but she had not left it before she had succeeded in standing as a copper snake and totem figure for the natives. Now she was at the point when her artistic accomplishment had been completed with *Last Tales*, which, while not her last book, was the one that represented her final spiritual victory and placed a seal on her poisonously powerful oeuvre. Now a new dimension of existence is in the process of gaining control over her consciousness, the monstrous elemental world of nocturnal dream, where "long perspectives stretch before me, distance is the password of the scenery, at times I feel that the fourth dimension is within reach. I fly, in dream, to any altitude, I dive into bottomless, clear, bottle-green waters."

About this universe of dream she writes as one who knows it well and in a way that is consistent with the underlying philosophy in her tales:

For we have in the dream forsaken our allegiance to the organizing, controlling and rectifying forces of the world, the Universal Conscience. We have sworn fealty to the wild, incalculable, creative forces, the Imagination of the Universe. . . . To the imagination of the world we do not pray. . . . Without our having asked them for freedom, these free forces have set us free as mountain winds, have liberated us from initiative and determination, as from responsibility. They deal out no wages, each of their boons to us is a gift, baksheesh, and their highest gift is inspiration. . . . . The ship has given up tacking and has allied herself with the wind and the current; now her sails fill and she runs on, proudly, upon obliging waves. (P. 477)

Now, as she faces her life's conclusion, she feels the center of gravity of her existence shifting once again, and she is prepared and already filled with longing for the final, unconditional surrender:

Already now I feel, as when at the age of twenty I was going to a ball in the evening, that day is a space of time without meaning, and that it is with the coming of dusk, with the lighting of the first star and the first candle, that things will become what they really are, and will come forth to meet me. (P. 477)

Remembering her way of walking in her final years, one can see her with uncertain, swaying steps, as if against waves, moving into the night which is shining for her, and taking possession of it like a queen.

## 3.

One more section is required in this afterword. It would be about the panic that sometimes strikes the narrators in Karen Blixen's tales. This happens, among others, to Mira Jama in "The Diver," when with consternation he discovers that the story he has composed about the Sultan from Shiraz turns out to be true, real, for he meets him in person: "It is a terrible experience for a storyteller to discover that his story is true. I was young, a novice in my art, the hair rose up on my head, and I was on the point of getting up and running away."

What the incident suggests is that if a person has the strength and perseverance to go to the outermost limits of consciousness, then the customary distinctions of ordinary language dissolve and things no longer maintain themselves within their ascribed definitions; rather, their opposites break forth from them.

But this is a section I cannot write. Someone else will have to do it when time and the occasion render it possible.